No AYC 106, Albion Victor
type PK115 with Thomas
Harrington 26-seat coachwork.
It is seen parked at
Malmsmead whilst operating a
Lynmouth and Doone Valley
Tour. The Driver is Mr Peter
Quinn, July 1938. *Photo
courtesy The Jersey Evening
Post.*

THE
BLUE MOTORS
Remembered

Roy H. Lee

Roadmaster Publishing

First published in 1994 by
ROADMASTER PUBLISHING,
1 Polhill Drive, Walderslade,
Chatham, Kent ME5 9PN

© Roy H. Lee 1994

ISBN 1-871814-51-0

British Library Cataloguing-in-Publication Data
A catalogue record for this book is available
from the British Library.

Typeset by Vitaset, Paddock Wood, Kent
Printed in Great Britain by Biddles Ltd,
Guildford, Surrey

Contents

Author's Notes

My life started at Brent Knoll, Somerset during 1936, and as a boy of about ten I travelled to Minehead on several occasions by train. My interest in the Blue Motors started after leaving the railway station, for there were usually one or two of their vehicles waiting on the other side of the approach road. Their dark blue livery and immaculate condition always impressed me, so I decided to find out more about them. Over the years my knowledge grew, leading eventually to this book.

My main occupations have involved me in costing with a British Aircraft subsidiary and in selling with a motor accessory firm.

Acknowledgements

I should like to thank the many people who have supplied information to make this book possible. In particular I should like to acknowledge the help of Mr Charlie Babb, the Company Foreman, who was always willing to spare time to answer my queries, and for his kindness in giving me permission to reproduce many of his pre-war photographs. To Mrs R M Read, a niece of Mr W Manley, from whom I purchased a collection of pre-war photographs. To Mr Eric Tarr who provided his photograph taken outside of the Minehead office and to Mr Sid Ward for his photographs, including the one of the holiday tour people, and his help with some of my queries. Mrs M Freegard for the loan of her photograph of Mr Francis Freegard and to Mrs Joan Astell for the photograph of the rear view of the Daimler char-a-banc. To Mr Dennis Corner of Porlock Museum for the photograph of the waggonette and to Mrs M Freeman-Archer of The West Somerset Museum, Allerford. Mr W J Carman for a copy of his 1934 timetable and also the following people who helped with my queries: Mr Ernest Bowden, Mr Bill Martin, Mrs Sybil Woodman (nee Wood), Mrs V M Gill, Mrs M Charlebois, Miss Nellie Blackmore, Mrs K Willis, Mr Edgar Ward. Also to Gordon Richmond, L F Folkard, G V Bruce, D I Grey, G W Watts and R Polley of the PSV Circle, R G Westgate of the Omnibus Society, D M M Shorrocks and the staff of the Somerset Record Office, Mrs S M Johnson of the Western Traffic Area office, Bristol and to the staff of the now former local Taxation offices of the Somerset County Council, and the City of Bristol. Finally to the Jersey Evening Post.

Also reproduced are a selection of my post-war Blue Motors photographs.

Introduction

The Porlock Weir, Porlock and Minehead Motor Service Company Limited and especially its fleet name of Blue Motors were well known for over forty years in the Minehead and Porlock area of Somerset. It was a company which was started by local people, as shareholders, for local people, mainly as its title suggests to operate a bus service between the little harbour village of Porlock Weir, the picturesque village of Porlock, and the town of Minehead. In an area of particular beauty on the edge of Exmoor, and much supported by holiday makers during the summer months, its splendid buses, char-a-bancs and coaches were always maintained to such a high standard, in particular their gleaming dark blue paintwork was always kept immaculate. Their vehicles could also be seen at many places in the West Country operating coach tours, and in parts of Wales and Scotland on holiday tours.

Mr F J Stoate managed and was secretary to the Company for thirty years. He was greatly respected by the staff and many other people in the area, along with Mr Charlie Babb who was Engineer and Foreman to the Company for over thirty years.

In my research for information for this book I spoke to many people and everywhere I went, whether it was the local Taxation Office at Taunton, or visiting local people at places in West Somerset, they all remembered the Blue Motors and spoke well of them. It is now over thirty years since they amalgamated with the other Minehead coach firm, the Scarlet Pimpernel Coaches, to form a new company during April 1954.

I have happy memories of the Blue Motors and their staff and I hope that this book will act as a remembrance to them. It should also be of interest to my fellow bus enthusiasts and give future generations an insight into the practises showing how a bus and coach company worked in those early days.

R H LEE
Brent Knoll, Somerset.
September 1991

1

Early Days to 1939

During 1916 a company was formed at Minehead in Somerset, to acquire the bus part of the business of Messrs Hardy and Company, of The Avenue, Minehead, who were operating a bus service between Porlock Weir and Minehead. On 19 May 1916 the new company was registered with the title of the Porlock Weir, Porlock and Minehead Motor Service Company Limited, with the registered office at 3 Friday Street, Minehead, Somerset. The secretary was Mr F J Loveless. On 4 January 1917 the Manager and Secretary was Mr Thomas Priscott and from about 1922 the registered office was at 25 The Avenue, Minehead (later re-numbered to 39 The Avenue). The Company purchased Messrs Hardy and Company's bus service and one vehicle, but they continued on with the haulage side of their business. In these early days the Company kept most of its vehicles in its well built garage at Quirke Street, Minehead, which could accommodate up to at least eight, and possibly ten char-a-bancs. Later some of these were replaced by small 20-seat coaches. It was during 1935 that the North Road garage replaced these premises, which were then sold. From about 1920 the Company operated with the fleet name of Blue Motors.

At Porlock Weir the Company also had a small garage (situated on the right hand side of the road as one enters the village), this was just before the start of the sea wall which housed the service bus used to operate the regular journeys to Minehead. There were no petrol pumps, an outside lavatory was provided, along with some lock up garages in a yard behind, but these were not used to house their vehicles.

In the village of Porlock the Company had a small office, with a telephone, which was on one side of quite a large bus shelter surrounded by seats. It was situated at the west end of the village, on the present site of Messrs Pollard's showroom. Mr Frank Norman who lived in Rose Cottage next door, used to deal with bookings at this office, which was used until about 1935/6 when it was taken down. (The bus shelter was removed to the recreation ground and used as a cricket pavilion.)

A view of the garage at Quirke Street, Minehead, taken during 1967, long after the Blue Motors had moved to North Road.

The office was replaced by another at Porlock alongside Messrs Leith's café where a coach was sometimes parked. These premises were on the right hand side of the road, looking towards Porlock Weir, but it is not certain if the Company owned these premises. After the 1939 War bookings were taken at the Central Garage.

The Blue Motors operated their bus service keeping to the main A39 road between Porlock Weir and Minehead, (via the fairly large village of Porlock, Newbridge for Horner Woods, which are situated away on the right; the village of Allerford, Budleigh Hill for Selworthy, Brakeley Steps for Luccombe, the top of Woodcombe Lane, Minehead, then on through the town to the railway station approach). It was much later on that some journeys went via the village of Bossington. Before the motor vehicles of Messrs Hardy and Company, the route had been operated by horse brakes.

The Company bought a service bus to operate the bus service, and some char-a-bancs which were used to operate tours and outings. In addition they also operated motor cars for Private Hire.

A firm registered as Hardy Central Garage Ltd

A view of the garage at Porlock Weir, one can just see the sea on the extreme left of the picture.

operated a bus service during the 1920s to Lynton. This firm were also general hauliers and their premises were at The Avenue, Minehead on the site from where the Western National Omnibus Company Limited operated. These premises were on the opposite side of the Avenue further along in the Porlock direction from the Blue Motors office (now Leo's store). This firm later bought a firm called Colwills of Bideford, Devon, which became Messrs Hardy-Colwills. They covered a large area of bus operation, mainly in Devon, and subsequently this firm was bought by the then National Omnibus and Transport Company Limited, whose registered offices were in London. (This Company was already operating a bus service between Minehead and Bridgwater prior to their purchase of Messrs Hardy-Colwills' business.) Later on the National Company was split up into areas and Minehead was in the area covered by the Western National Omnibus Company, whose registered offices were at Exeter.

A certain Mr E Ford who lived at Alcombe, near Minehead, also decided to operate vehicles along the Minehead-Porlock Weir road, in competition with the Blue Motors. He traded as Mascot Motors. His fleet in

15

yellow livery included a 20-seat Reo, a 26-seat AJS and a Chevrolet seating 14 passengers. One of his vehicles would be driven to Porlock, then wait there, setting off for Minehead just before the Blue Motors' vehicle came up from Porlock Weir, and running a few minutes in front of it to pick up the passengers first. His fares were lower, resulting in the Blue Motors reducing their fares. This continued until about 1931 when Mr Ford sold his business to the Western National Omnibus Company. Now there were the Blue Motors and the Western National vehicles operating along the Porlock road in competition with each other.

At first the livery for Y 4265, the Karrier bus, was brown and buff, and Y 6187, the Daimler char-a-banc, was brown. From about 1920 the livery was a rich dark blue all over, except for some vehicles which pre-war were dark blue below (and including the waistline) and white above it. These few vehicles were service buses and the two colours were to distinguish them from the remainder of the fleet. The only relief to the dark blue livery of the pre-war coaches being the line or moulding along the sides under the windows. This was usually polished chrome or a similar surface, being silver in colour. On coaches delivered after the war years this moulding was painted light blue (although two of the Bedford SB coaches had polished lines). After 1944 the service buses were also in the dark blue all over livery with a light blue line around the waistline. Some coaches had a white background to the front and rear glass plates, these being lettered in blue, but usually both coaches and buses had a dark blue background with white lettering to these plates. On the rear panel of most of the coaches and buses was the oval sign of the Company painted in gold, made up of two oval-shaped lines one inside of the other, with the names Porlock Weir between the lines on the top curve and Minehead between the lines of the lower curve. These were written in capital letters and inside the inner oval line were the words 'Blue Motors' written in a copperplate script. Mr Walter Knight was the signwriter who did this painting.

The first vehicle owned by the Company was registered Y 401. The history of this particular registration number is rather unusual. According to the Vehicle Registration Ledgers of the Somerset County Council the number was first issued on 21 July 1905 to Mr William John Hippersley of New Street, Wells, Somerset, for an 8-10 hp Humber Coventry car. It was transferred on 21 August 1908 to a char-a-banc (no details given) licenced to Messrs Sampson Jones, High Street, Wells, Somerset. It was cancelled on 13 May 1914 and was re-issued again on 20 May 1914, again to Messrs Sampson Jones, for a Napier 25 hp char-a-banc painted stone grey in colour with a weight 2 tons 10 cwt 3 qrs. The axle weight of each axle: (front) 1 ton 7 cwt 1 qr, (rear) 3 tons. Wheel size was 33 ins in diameter and the solid rubber tyres were: front single 2 in wide and rear double 2 in wide. It was transferred to Messrs Hardy and Company on 1 July 1915. The ledger gives the registration as being cancelled on 19 April 1916 with the note: 'Y 401 assigned to another char-a-banc the property of Hardy & Co'. In another separate entry further on Y 401 is given as being issued on 19 April 1916 to Messrs Hardy & Co, per James Hardy, 'Beechcroft', The Avenue, Minehead, for a Napier 25 hp, Public Bus, Mahogany (Colour), with 22 seats, weight 2 tons 12 cwt. The axle weight of each axle being: (front) 1 ton 7 cwt, (rear) 3 tons, a wheel size of 33 in in diameter, and the solid rubber tyres were: (front) single 4 in wide and rear twin 6 in wide. I remember asking Mr Charlie Babb, the Company Engineer and Foreman, (who joined the Company in the early days for he was with them by 1920), what type of vehicle the Napier was? He told me that it was a char-a-banc, and had come from Messrs Hardy & Co. and Mr Edgar Ward also remembered a Napier char-a-banc in the fleet. This would appear to be borne out by the weight of it (2 tons 12 cwt would seem to be rather light for a 22 seat vehicle with a bus body). In addition the note about Y 401 being assigned to a char-a-banc would support this. The 6 June 1916 was the date of the transfer of the Napier to the new Company. It was withdrawn from service during August 1919, parts of its bodywork when it was dismantled being built on to the bodywork of Karrier bus Y 4265.

The next vehicle to be registered on 15 July 1916 was Y 4318, a Maudslay 25/30 hp vehicle. It is described as a 'passenger carrying vehicle' with a 'waggonette type of body', its colour was mahogany. No seating capacity is given in the records. From a photograph of a waggonette it would appear to have sat 11 passengers, had seats around the sides, and a hood which folded up together in the front of it behind the driver, thus leaving room for passengers to come aboard or leave it at the rear. The weight was 19 cwt 1 qr. A Karrier 50 hp bus Y 4265 was the next vehicle to be registered on 20 July 1916. The

17

This picture is of particular interest as it shows the Porlock Girl Guides about to set off for Lynmouth about 1920. I have confirmation that it was a Company vehicle and the driver was Mr Everett. It would appear to be Y 4318, a Maudslay 25/30 hp waggonette, which appears to have wooden sides. Its colour was registered as mahogany (note the hood is folded up behind the driver, and not at the rear). The original print is in Porlock Museum and it is reproduced here by courtesy of Mr Dennis Corner, the curator.

registration entry gives it as having a commercial chassis, and a station bus body. The colour was brown and buff, weight 4 tons 8 cwt 2 qrs, axle weight of each axle: (front) 2 tons 10 cwt, (rear) 4 tons 15 cwt. The diameter of wheels: (front) 900 mm, (rear) 1050 mm, and the width and material of tyres width (front) single 120 mm, (rear) double 120 mm rubber. There is an interesting note pencilled in on the entry which reads: 'Copy entry sent to General Accident, Fire and Life Assurance Corporation Ltd, 13 Clare Street, Bristol, 20-1-17'. It had solid looking hard top bodywork with a rail running around near the edge on the top of the roof, so that luggage could be placed up there. At the front there were two windscreens placed next to each other, with the bonnet projected well out in front of them, and the Karrier name on the top of the front of the radiator grille. Inside it had a rather unusual layout being divided into two parts, the front part had four rows of leather seats right across it, (each row had its own entrance door) the rear part had wooden seats around it, the entrance to this part was at the back of the bus, outside

Karrier bus Y 4265. (Note the fairly long bonnet, and the first entrance door near the front. Note also that the headlamps are lower down than in another view.) The driver is Mr Tom Bowden who drove this bus for a number of years. A view taken near the Railway Station at Minehead.

of which there was a platform built. The passengers climbed up some steps and once inside the entrance turned to the left. Sometimes the conductor would stand outside on the platform. There was also a ladder attached to the back to get up to the roof. It accomodated 35 passengers and was by 1921 repainted in an all dark blue livery being later operated in the dark blue below, and white above the waistline livery. In those days the vehicles were given names, this one was *King of the Road*. The name was painted along on the front below the windscreens. This bus was used to operate the bus service journeys and was well known and loved.

On 4 January 1917 a car was registered to the Company. It was Y 2573, a Ford 20 hp, 4 seater, with a weight of 15 cwt. Its colour was black and was new to Mr John Wallis Willis, of Prospect House, Porlock, Somerset. He had first registered it on 18 June 1914 but by the time it went to its next owners, after the Company sold it, the colour had been changed to brown. On 31 March 1920 it was transferred to Messrs Yandle and Sons Ltd of Silver Street, Ilminster, Somerset, and then on the same date it was transferred to Mr Tom Parris of the George Inn, Chardstock, Chard, Somerset. Then there was Y 4618 an Austin 25 hp char-a-banc seating 18 passengers, which was registered on 18 May 1917. It had the following details: a weight of 3 tons 2 qrs, the axle weight of each axle being (front) 1 ton 14 cwt, (rear) 4 tons 5 cwt. All the wheels were 34 ins diameter and the solid rubber tyres were: (front) single 4 in wide, (rear) twin 8 in wide. Where it asks 'For use as a public conveyance' it has 'Yes and HM Mails' written in. There were a pair of windscreens fitted across the front and the engine was under a curved bonnet, (the front of which sloped away downwards, getting slightly wider as it curved down to the chassis). This char-a-banc was named *Duchess*. As with other char-a-bancs the name was not painted on the front, it would have been displayed on the back. On 28 February 1919 the Company registered Y 5265, a Ford 15 hp car and its

Karrier char-a-banc Y 7665 at Cheddar. (Note the owner's nameplate which mentions speed – 12 miles per hour.) The vehicle has solid tyres and the driver is Mr Charlie Babb.

weight is given as 'under 1 ton', the colour was black. This was followed by a larger looking char-a-banc which was fairly high off the ground, a Daimler 22 hp, registered Y 6187 on 29 August 1919. It had the following details: an unladen weight 3 tons 8 cwt 3 qrs, the axle weight of each axle being: (front) 1 ton 14 cwt, (rear) 4 tons 5 cwt. All the wheels were 34 ins in diameter, and the solid rubber tyres were: (front) single 3½ in wide and (rear) twin 8 in wide. Its colour was brown. As with the other char-a-bancs it had a large fabric hood which on fine days was folded up at the back with its supports all placed neatly in position, extending out over the rear of the vehicle. If the weather was wet it would be pulled forward until it was attached to the top of the windscreen, with its supports in position at the sides to keep the hood up above the passenger heads. There were several doors along one side (the side opposite to the driver), with each row of seats going right across the vehicle having its own door. This particular char-a-banc had two running boards along under the doors for the passengers to use to step up into it. The accommodation was for 23 passengers and the name

This photograph was taken circa 1920 and shows some of the vehicles lined up before starting on an outing. They are parked opposite the Minehead Post Office on the road towards Porlock. The vehicles are Y 4265, the Karrier service bus, and char-a-bancs Y 4618 Austin, Y 6187 Daimler, and Y 7665 Karrier. The Manager of the Company, Mr T Priscott, is standing by the service bus.

This interesting photograph is of the Daimler char-a-banc Y 6187, showing a view of the rear and one side of it with the hood up. The name of it, *The Empress*, is painted on the rear panel with the words PORLOCK MINEHEAD. (Note the Hackney Carriage plate above the rear number plate, and the rod from the top of the windscreen to the mudguard; this was later removed.) The picture appears to be a bodybuilder's advertisement '25 seater char-a-banc by A G Dowell Exeter' being written on the print. In actual fact it carried 23 passengers after it entered service. It is reproduced here by courtesy of Joan Astell.

given to it was *The Empress*. The bonnet projected well out in front with the Daimler name written in script type writing along the top of the radiator. Its bodywork was built by A G Dowell of Exeter. It was usual for Daimler vehicles at this time to be fitted with a Knight 4-cylinder 22.4 hp, sleeve valve petrol engine.

Then came Y 8858 an overland 16-20 hp car, a landaulette, it would have had a folding roof which when pulled back would open up. It was registered on 29 July 1920, its weight was 1 ton 16 cwt and the colour was green.

A 50 hp Karrier char-a-banc seating 28 persons was next, Y 7665, it was registered on 9 August 1920 and had an unladen weight of 4 tons 8 cwt 2 qrs, the axle weight of each axle being: (front) 2 tons 10 cwt, (rear) 5 tons. Its wheels: (front) 2 ft 10 ins diameter, (rear) 3 ft 4 in diameter, with solid rubber tyres: (front) single 4½ in wide, (rear) twin 9 in wide. Its colour is given as blue. The bodywork was larger in appearance than the previous two, and had the usual fabric hood. Again the bonnet was projected well out in front, and the radiator grille was of the same design as the one on the first Karrier but was slightly narrower. This vehicle was given the name *Queen of the West*. All the char-a-bancs up until now had solid tyres, but this one was later fitted

22

Karrier XB 9780, parked outside of the garage at Quirke Street, Minehead, after it had pneumatic tyres fitted.

with pneumatic tyres. In a photograph one can see that the Daimler and this Karrier each had a curved plate attached to the top of the front number plate with the words 'Hackney Carriage' written on them. Up until this time the char-a-bancs had been restricted to a speed of 12 miles per hour – this is mentioned on each entry in the Vehicle Registration ledgers for them. Also owned was another Karrier char-a-banc, XB 9780, which appears to have accommodated 28 passengers, and is seen in one photograph as having solid tyres when it entered service. These were later replaced by new wheels and pneumatic tyres. The bodywork was similar to that on the earlier char-a-bancs, one of which was named *Princess*, but it is not known which one it was.

It was during 1921 that Mr Tom Priscott, who was then the Manager of the Company, was succeeded by Mr F J Stoate, who held the position of Manager and Secretary of the Company for the next thirty years. He had previously been the Company Secretary of Messrs Staddon & Sons of Friday Street, Minehead, who were also motor car and char-a-banc operators.

At about this time the registered office was changed from 3 Friday Street, to 25 The Avenue, Minehead (later re-numbered by 1949 to 39 The Avenue, owing to a general re-numbering of premises there). The building

A general view of one of the Crossley char-a-bancs.

consisted of a general booking office, and another private office behind which had a separate entrance door from outside and a passage-way along the side of the general office as well as an inside door between the two offices. There was a forecourt outside on which a vehicle was usually parked, to advertise the tours, in addition to the usual advertisement boards. A bus service timetable was displayed on a board on a post at the right hand side of the forecourt by the Avenue footpath.

During 1922 YA 2828, YA 3077 and YA 4003, three Crossley 25 hp, 14-seat char-a-bancs entered service. Each body was fitted with a canvas hood; the chassis had been previously purchased from the Government and were believed to have been ex War Department. Later they had bodywork fitted. The standard engine for the 25 hp Crossley chassis supplied to the Government was a 4½ litre 4-cylinder side valve engine.

Also owned was another Karrier with a char-a-banc body fitted, but this one was different in its seating arrangements, seats being placed in rows across the vehicle. But instead of all facing foward they were arranged back to back. The passengers entered the vehicle by the usual side entrances and then could sit on either of two seats, one facing forward and the other facing towards the back. When the vehicle was withdrawn from service this char-a-banc was sold and

24

YA 6600, a Lancia char-a-banc. This photograph is believed to have been taken during 1924.

delivered to a firm of showmen at Bristol. The next known vehicle to arrive was YA 6600, a 19-seat Lancia. This vehicle and the Lancia which arrived later on, were bought from agents, Messrs Alldays of London. It is interesting to note that at first a photograph of the vehicle was sent to the Blue Motors and I was told the decision to purchase was based entirely on this photograph. On 25 July 1923, YA 6600 was registered. It had a char-a-banc body with the usual individual doors fitted and had a large hood, with an unladen weight of 2 tons 8½ cwt. The bodybuilders' name is not known and, according to the Somerset County Council records, the chassis was older than its registration date and had been previously owned by the War Department.

It was on 27 April 1926 that two Albion, type PN 26, 'Open' 26-seater coaches were registered, these being YB 5914 and YB 5915. They were both collected from Messrs Harris of Bristol, who had built the bodywork on them. Inside they had two rows of double seats with a central gangway in between. There was a single front entrance and a large hood was fitted, which on fine days could be folded back behind the rear seat like the ones on the char-a-bancs. The windscreens were placed forming a forward facing V shape and the 30 hp engine was under a bonnet projected out in front, this type

YB 5914, an Albion type PN 26 with 'Open' coach Harris of Bristol bodywork. It is in its original condition, and is seen crossing through the water at Malmsmead.

being known as a normal control layout, ie the driver is sitting behind the engine as opposed to sitting alongside of it (the forward control layout). I was told that after some time these two open coaches were overhauled and windows were fitted along the sides. These may have been detachable but this is not certain and with the hood pulled over if required, it would make for a much more comfortable journey. Next to arrive was YC 599, an Albion, type PK 26 model of 30/60 hp, fitted with a 4-cylinder petrol engine. It was registered on 27 July 1927 and had 29-seat front entrance bodywork built by Duple. By the mid 1930s the seating capacity had been reduced to 26. This bus was known as *The Warrior* and on the registration papers the description is given as 'Saloon Bus', being painted in the livery of dark blue below the waistline and white above it. A second Lancia arrived next, YC 3473, which had a 35 hp engine. I was told that it was a char-a-banc seating 20 passengers. Following this the first Dennis was delivered, it was a GL type, YC 7355. It would have been fitted with a 3.77 litre 6-cylinder Dennis petrol engine and had 20-seat bus bodywork built by Duple with a front entrance. Like the previous Albion bus, it had the emergency door in the centre at the back. This Dennis was registered on 26 August 1929 and was operated by Mr Bill Manley who at the time drove it, collected the fares, and issued the tickets on it. (There being no conductor carried, this was an early example of one man operation!)

By now two Armstrong Siddeley cars had been placed in service, both having HU registration letters. One, the number part of which is not known, was, during 1929 struck and damaged by a falling tree on the main road at St Audries. Mr Charlie Babb was the driver and this car was then withdrawn from use. The other Armstrong Siddeley HU 8108 was licenced to carry eight persons. A regular use for one of the best cars was to convey the Reverend Parry Liddon, who at the time was the Vicar of Minehead, about on Sundays, whilst Mr Charlie Babb acted as chauffeur.

At sometime Mr Charlie Babb suggested to the management that the firm start operating a bus service to Taunton, but they decided against this stating that it might upset the Great Western Railway officials, whose trains ran to Taunton. They could have stopped their vehicles using the railway station approach at Minehead, and the Company would not have wanted that to happen.

The Road Traffic Act came into being during 1930, and subsequently the Company were licensed to operate their stage carriage service between Porlock Weir and Minehead. As mentioned earlier, Mr E Ford, later Western National, was also licensed to operate along the same route, and at this time both firms operated separately from each other. An excursions and tours licence was issued to the Company to operate coach tours from Minehead and Porlock which included various other picking up points in the area. Similar excursions and tours licences were also granted to Messrs Hawkins Bros (who had operated the Scarlet Pimpernel coaches from Minehead since 1922), and also to the Western National Omnibus Co Ltd. So it was fairly competitive in operating coach tours in the area.

On 20 April 1932 a large capacity service bus was licensed. This was a forward control type with the driver's cab alongside the engine. The new bus, YD 4593, was a Dennis Lancet 1, having a 30 hp engine and fitted with 32-seat rear entrance bodywork built by Duple. It had a full width roof canopy, (that is to say the roof came out square covering the area opposite the driver's cab) with a single destination box at the front, above which an oval-shaped sign with the Blue Motors' name on it was suspended over part of the roof, and attached to it by a bracket on each side of it. On the rear

YD 4593, a Dennis Lancet, parked at the departure place, Porlock Weir. The driver is Mr W Manley, and the conductor is Mr Alf Fowler.

A side view of YD 4593 showing the luggage carrier on the roof. This bus had 32-seat bodywork built by Duple. The crew are the same two men named above.

part of the roof was a luggage container. There was a straight band a few inches wide running along under the windows which had PORLOCK WEIR PORLOCK MINEHEAD written along it. There were also some curtains inside pulled together at the side-window pillars and fastened to them at the centre of each. During May 1932, YD 4700, a Dennis Dart with a 3.77 litre 6-cylinder Dennis petrol engine, was placed in service. It had 20-seat front entrance bodywork built by Duple and was a coach which was withdrawn during May 1936 and sold to Messrs Hawkins Bros (Scarlet Pimpernel Coaches) of Minehead. The registration number itself is interesting in that Sir William Meade-King of Walford House, West Monkton, Somerset, wanted YD 4700 for his new Morris Oxford car, and requested it from the Somerset County Council licencing department. A letter was sent to him on 2 December 1930 informing him that the registration number would not be available for several months and offered him YD 47 and YD 70. He replied on 3 December 1930 accepting YD 47. During May 1933, YD 7169, Albion Victor, type PH 49, with 20-seat Duple coachwork was registered. A year later on 11 May 1934, YD 9697, another Dennis Lancet 1 was registered. Having 32-seat front entrance body-work, again built by Duple, along with a full width canopy, this time there was a small destination box over the cab front, and a matching panel with the Blue Motors' name painted on alongside it. A luggage container was carried on the rear part of the roof and there was also a straight band along under the windows without any lettering on it. On some occasions, if required (although I understand these were fairly rare), this bus was used to operate some coach tours and, together with the 1932 one making a pair, were the main ones used to operate the service journeys during the remaining part of the 1930s. Both were painted in the service bus livery of dark blue below the waistline, including the straight band along under the windows, and white above it.

At this time these two Dennis Lancet service buses were kept at the Porlock Weir garage as most of the stage carriage service shifts were worked from this end of the route. Originally the Karrier bus *King of the Road* was kept there, with sometimes a char-a-banc to help out on service journeys. It was replaced there during July 1927 by YC 599, the Albion PK 26, Duple-bodied 29-seat bus. Some of the drivers and conductors lived

YD 9697 was a Dennis Lancet 1, with 32-seat Duple bodywork. It is seen in the pre-war bus livery of dark blue below and white above the waistline. The driver is Mr Charlie Babb. (Note that he has an original oval shape driver's badge displayed.)

It was early 1935 when the North Road Garage was opened. This is a view of the front.

locally and had to go to this garage to start the morning journeys to Minehead. Among them was Mr Tom Bowden of Porlock, who had earlier taken on driving *King of the Road* from Mr Frank Radford, its first driver. Mr Bowden rode his motor bike to work in the 1930s. His conductor was Mr Victor Manley, whose brother was driver Mr Bill Manley, who also worked from there. He had several conductors at different times working with him including Mr Alf Fowler, Mr Sid Ward and Mr Ernie Bowden, Mr Tom Bowden's son, who when he had left school started work as office boy at the Company office at Porlock. He was promoted to conductor and rode his cycle from Porlock to work at Porlock Weir. Later on, after the war, he became a driver. There were only two drivers and two conductors at a time working from Porlock Weir garage with each pair working each bus all day long, six days a week. They worked very long hours which went on until 1940 when the war-time cut backs changed all this. Mr Ernie Bowden's dinner was brought to the Minehead garage for him to eat during his dinner break. There was also a relief crew, driver Mr Dick Boyle and conductor Mr Sid Ward, who operated YC 599, the Albion, Duple-bodied bus, on duplicate journeys.

During June 1934 the first Lancia char-a-banc YA 6600 was withdrawn. The new garage at North Road, Minehead, was opened early in 1935. This extremely well-built garage had an attractive front built of a brownish stone, with high dark blue painted wooden doors which were made up of vertical sections hinged together making a pair which opened in opposite directions, set back inwards a few feet from the road. Extending out to the road on each side of these there was incorporated on one side an office for the garage Foreman, and on the other side a matching room which I believe to be the Staff room. These office walls are built upwards and joined across the top above the entrance thus completing the outside appearance. The fleet was well housed here, the inside including a well equipped service bay at the far end, two inspection pits, and an area for paint spraying. This garage replaced the Quirke Street garage. Drivers, especially in the winter, would help out with any maintenance work in the garage. Drivers had half a day each week for maintaining their vehicle, 'Simonize' wax polish was used on them, polishing a panel each day. The first vehicles to be delivered to the new garage were a pair of Albion

Victor, type PK 115 coaches, AYC 106 and AYC 107. These had 26-seat coachwork, with a centre entrance, built by Thomas Harrington of Hove, Sussex, to their half cab design. They were fitted with 4-cylinder Albion 3.88 litre petrol engines with $3\frac{3}{4}$ in × $5\frac{3}{8}$ in size cylinders. These were followed by two more Albion coaches, firstly BYC 341, a 20-seat Victor, type PK 115, then shortly after by BYC 698, a Valkyrie with 30-seats, both of these also had centre entrance coachwork built by Thomas Harrington Ltd.

It is interesting to note that Armstrong Siddeley car HU 8108, and PJ 3299, believed to have been the Austin Taxi which was referred to as the 'Big Austin', were both during part of the 1930s issued with a PSV licence. It is not known why this was so, as no one I have spoken to about this can remember either of them being used on the bus service journeys.

It appears that during the 1930s the Company had a fairly prosperous time and more new vehicles arrived. On 28 July 1936 a Dennis Lancet, type 2, 32-seat coach was registered. The coachwork was built by Dennis Bros Ltd. On the registration papers this coach is described as a 'Sun Saloon'. It was BYD 178, having a 35.7 hp engine. During September 1936 the second Lancia, YC 3473 was withdrawn from service. The next vehicle to be delivered was CYB 715, a Leyland Lion LT7 model, having 28-seat coachwork built by Thomas Harrington, of the type as supplied to the previous four Albions but with a front entrance. It had a glass panel along each side extending from above the front window and along for a few feet below the curve of the roof. On this panel were painted the words 'Observation Coach' or 'Blue Motors Observation Coach'. On the one I remember seeing, which was on BYC 341, the writing was in blue on a white background. This particular vehicle was lettered 'Observation Coach'. CYB 715, had a 5.9 litre petrol engine with 4 cylinders of $4\frac{9}{16}$ in bore and $5\frac{1}{2}$ in stroke, and was later fitted with new coachwork by the same coachbuilder.

An AEC Regal was registered on 31 May 1937. This was CYC 463. As the chassis number didn't start with an O (for an oil engine), it would have had a 6.1 litre AEC 6-cylinder petrol engine fitted, and had coachwork by Thomas Harrington seating 32 passengers. On the registration papers it is described as an 'Observation Saloon', having the style of coachwork mentioned previously, and had the words 'Blue Motors

CYC 463 was an AEC Regal with Thomas Harrington 32-seat coachwork which was new during 1937. The destination blind is set at Tarr Steps. Driver is Mr Charlie Babb.

Observation Coaches' written in white on a dark blue background on the glass plate along the sides above the windows. This vehicle had a front entrance and a thin chrome line along its waistline. Just over halfway back on the sides, the actual line of the coachwork along under the windows is stepped up a few inches, as are the windows above it, thus also raising the level of the top of these windows as compared with the remainder. Down the centre of the roof this coach was fitted with a wide strip of fabric-type material, which during the warm weather could be folded back towards the rear of the roof. I understand that this style of coachwork was fitted to Albions AYC 106, BYC 341 and BYC 698, and also to Leyland CYB 715, and most likely to Albion AYC 107.

DYC 20 was delivered next, this was a Leyland Cheetah. This coach had a new and very attractive style of coachwork seating 31 passengers. The roof lines swept well down towards the rear end giving a swept tail appearance, and made more interesting by the addition of a dorsal fin. This housed an air duct to ventilate the coach, and also quarter roof light windows were fitted along each side on the curve of the roof. Down the centre of the roof there was a wide strip of fabric type material which, when a handle situated behind the

DYC 20 was a Leyland Cheetah, with 27-seat coachwork built by Thomas Harrington. A close look will reveal the fleet number 1 fixed on the side of the bonnet. The coach is seen at Burnham-on-Sea on a tour to Weston-super-Mare during 1952. The driver is Mr J H Day.

driver in the cab was turned, would fold back towards the rear of the roof. At the end of this it would form folds creased upwards. DYC 20 had a thin chrome line along its waistline and at the rear two glass plates were fitted, these being separated by the thin point of the dorsal fin which was moulded into the coachwork at this particular place. The two glass plates had one word painted on each, together they read 'Observation Coach', which was written in blue on a white background, as was the Blue Motors' name on the front glass plate. This coach was followed during August 1938 and March 1939 by two similar coaches, both accommodating 32 passengers; the only difference in the Thomas Harrington coachwork on these two being the side lines (having polished metal in between two thin strips making a wider moulding along the sides). They each had a Leyland 4.7 litre Light Six petrol engine with 3½ in bore and 5 in stroke cylinders. Later on during 1950 DYC 20 and EYA 923 had their seating capacity changed to 27 seats with EYB 488, the third one, having its seating capacity changed to accommodate 22 passengers.

During the previous years Blue Motors' vehicles carried fleet numbers which in earlier days were painted on by the Foreman. Later on, after the arrival of the half cab type vehicles, I noticed that small raised numbers were fixed to the bonnet side at the entrance end, those known are as follows: Albion open coach YB 5914 had the figure 12 painted on the fuel tank; YD 4593 Dennis

34

Leyland Cheetah EYA 923, parked in North Road, Minehead, waiting to operate a tour to Lynmouth and Doone Valley during July 1952.

Leyland Cheetah EYB 488, with Thomas Harrington coachwork, seen waiting to operate an afternoon tour to Quantock Hills during 1952.

Lancet was 7; BYC 341 Albion Victor was 6; CYC 463 AEC Regal was 14; and DYC 20 and EYA 923 Leyland Cheetah were 1 and 2 respectively. The use of these company fleet numbers appears to have been discontinued after the second Leyland Cheetah EYA 923. On checking the remaining one of this type, EYB 488, there was no sign of a number ever being fixed to its bonnet side.

2

The War Years and Post War Development

By the start of the wartime years, most of the earlier vehicles including YC 7355, the Dennis GL bus, had been withdrawn from service and sold. The company had sixteen buses, coaches and char-a-bancs licensed to them. There was also car HU 8108.

During September 1939 both of the Albion type PN 26 'Open' coaches YB 5914 and YB 5915 were withdrawn from service. The former was used as a Somerset County Council ambulance until December 1941 and the latter went to the Axbridge Rural District Council, becoming a fire tender which was subsequently withdrawn during December 1941. The Albion, YC 599, a type PK 26 service bus was also withdrawn during 1939, becoming a Somerset County Council ambulance eventually to be withdrawn during December 1943. The Albion Valkyrie coach, BYC 698, only just over three years old, was also withdrawn during September 1939, when it was requisitioned by the Government. During the same month there were many people evacuated from London and the South Coast. As they arrived by train at Minehead railway station Blue Motors' vehicles were lined up waiting to take them to local villages in the area, where a temporary home had been found for them.

It was also during 1939 that the Armstrong Siddeley Private Hire car HU 8108 was sold, the car hire side of the business not being resumed after the war.

During July 1940 the 1932 Dennis Lancet service bus YD 4593, was withdrawn from service. During the same month of that year a refund was made on the licence of the 1936 coach BYD 178, another Dennis Lancet. Both vehicles were requisitioned by the Government whilst the remaining Dennis Lancet service bus YD 9697 was also requisitioned during 1940.

The Government made a general request to Companies who were operating bus services along the same route as other licenced operators, suggesting that they operate the journeys jointly, presumably based on one timetable, thus saving the use of some vehicles and fuel. As a result the Company, and the Western

National Omnibus Co Ltd, started to operate the Minehead-Porlock Weir stage carriage service as a joint service, this joint arrangement continued to operate after the war years were over.

Some of the drivers were not now needed owing to the much reduced fleet, and there not being so much work to do as all coach tours were stopped. The men conductors were called up for military service and replaced by women conductresses, one was Mrs K Willis. The service journeys operated jointly were every two hours and the vehicles were often overcrowded with many standing passengers packed inside.

Between 1940 and 1946 the remaining coaches were used to operate the company's share of the journeys, these vehicles being fitted with a special shade on the front of the headlights. These had slits across them not to let too much light out, and so that they would not be seen from an enemy aircraft. In addition there was a white flash painted along the lower front part of each front mudguard.

Mrs Willis started her shift from Minehead North Road garage, she was conductress with driver Mr Tom Bowden, whom she always called 'Uncle Tom'. He also now started his shift from Minehead, and not from the Porlock Weir garage as he had previously done. So at least some, and possibly all, of the bus service staff worked from Minehead during the war years. She told me that in her earlier days, which would have been about this time, that the Blue Motors operated the morning journeys, and the Western National operated the afternoon journeys, one week at a time, then the following week they would change around working the system alternate weeks. During these years CYB 715, the Leyland Lion was one of the coaches used on service journeys. As well as the Leyland Cheetahs, she remembered that the roof inside of these Cheetahs sloped down fairly low towards the back. Mrs Willis also remembered that there were sometimes about three hundred people waiting for buses at the railway station approach at Minehead. She had to get off her coach and separate them so that the coach could turn around. As well as local people there were also many evacuees staying in the area. The conductresses could take the money taken on a duty home with them, count it there and enter the amount in their book, then pay it into the office later on.

There were journeys operated to take people who did

munitions work, from Minehead and other places en route to and from the Royal Ordnance factory at Puriton, near Bridgwater, a distance of over twenty-five miles each way. Several coaches were needed to operate them and these journeys were worked at a variety of times to suit the various shifts worked there.

The garage at North Road, Minehead was used for a time by the army, so the coaches were then kept in part of the Metropole garage, further along North Road, towards The Avenue.

YD 7169, the Albion Victor, type PH 49, coach was withdrawn during March 1942, and sold to Mr E G Bryant of Williton, Somerset.

During this time one new vehicle was delivered to the Company, this was a Bedford OWB with a 3.519 litre, 6-cylinder Bedford petrol engine, GYA 598, which had standard wartime utility bodywork built by Duple with 32 seats. These were later reduced to 30 seats and were of the wooden slatted type. This bus was painted in all dark blue livery, having a straight band several inches wide which went around it just under the windows, painted light blue with the company's fleet name painted in white on a dark blue background along the top of the destination indicator box. It was licensed during June 1944.

During July 1944, a refund was made on the licence of CYC 463, the AEC Regal coach, which was requisitioned by the Government.

After the war years, the Company owned eight or nine vehicles (depending whether Albion type PN 26, 'Open' coach YB 5915 was still owned or not, having been returned to the Company by 1945 and then withdrawn).

If they required them the Company had an option from the Government to purchase back the vehicles which had been requisitioned and they were particularly interested in re-purchasing the AEC Regal coach. The Company Foreman went to the Army Transport Department to inspect this one and the other vehicles, but found alterations had been made to suit the army requirements and it was decided not to re-purchase any of the vehicles. The Albion Valkyrie later went to Messrs Dodds and Company of Troon, Scotland, and the Foreman told me that the AEC Regal later went to a firm at or near Oxford.

There was a rise in wages for the staff: pre-war a driver was paid £2.0.0d a week, and a conductor £1.13.0d (£1.65p), this being for a six day week. A conductor was

AEC Regal HYB 676, with the Thomas Harrington 35-seat bodywork parked in North Road, Minehead. It is seen after operating a service journey from Porlock Weir on the afternoon of 11 June 1952.

known to have been paid an extra 6/– (30p) if he worked a Sunday shift. After the war years this went up to £2.10.0d (£2.50p) for a driver, this being increased sometime later on, by 1951, to £5.0.0d. It is not known what the rises for a conductor were at those times.

The first new vehicle to arrive after the war years was registered during December 1946, and was HYB 676 an AEC Regal with 7.7 litre AEC diesel engine with 6 cylinders of 4⅛ in bore and 5¾ in stroke. This was a service bus with 35-seat front entrance bodywork built by Thomas Harrington and it was very well built and finished. Inside it had a light fawn roof covering and blue upholstery, (which was dark with light part circles partly joined together). This patterned material was also used around the inside panelling from near the floor level up to just under the windows. The seat each side fitted over each rear mudguard was placed sideways to the others and these therefore faced each other. Externally it had a well proportioned appearance, with a light blue band which started on the side at the front corner, ran along the cab and right around the bus being carried over the entrance door to its finish. This bus with GYA 598, AYC 107, and AYC 106 (the latter being two Albion coaches) were seen working service journeys during a day in summer about 1947. During October 1947 a second new service bus was registered, JYB 168. This one was a Dennis Lancet, type J3, with a 7.6 litre 6-cylinder Dennis diesel engine, which also had 35-seat

Dennis Lancet JYB 168, with Thomas Harrington 35-seat bodywork. Seen (on 11 June 1952) at North Road, Minehead, having just come off a service journey from Porlock Weir.

front entrance bodywork built by Thomas Harrington, and was identical to the one on the AEC. This bus had a slightly wider light blue line around it. I remember these two buses had a printed card displayed inside on the centre of the bulkhead reading 'Notice, All dogs must be paid for and are not allowed on seats of bus, By Order.' These two buses were operated together as a pair on the Company's share of the stage service journeys, with the Bedford OWB (GYA 598) being used as duplicate when required in the summer months. It spent the winters stored in the Porlock Weir garage, out of use.

At this time all the stage service shifts were started from the Minehead end of the route, with the buses all being kept with the coaches at the North Road garage, Minehead. All the staff had to go there to collect their vehicles, the only exception was for coach driver Mr Sid Ward, who lived at Porlock. His allocated coach, firstly Leyland Cheetah (EYA 923) then from April 1948, Leyland Tiger PS1 (JYD 199) and from June 1950, Leyland Tiger PS2 (MYA 121) which he was successively in charge of, was occasionally kept overnight in the Porlock Weir garage, not now used for service buses. This was so that when required he could collect it in the morning, then set off for Minehead, picking up passengers en route who had booked to go on a coach tour from there. On arrival they would transfer to the coach waiting to operate the appropriate tour. He would then drive his coach on tours work during the day. After he returned to Minehead, the returning passengers from their coach tour would board his coach and he would set them down as he returned the coach to Porlock Weir garage for the night.

It is interesting to note that when one of the conductors, after his return from military service, and another man wanted to become drivers, they were asked to drive GYA 598, the Bedford OWB bus, to Porlock Weir and back, each taking a turn at driving, with Mr Charlie Babb on board, who if he was satisfied with their driving could say they were then regarded as drivers. This seems to have been all that was needed until about 1946 and I remember Mr Babb telling me that he sometimes went with learner drivers to Dunster Steep and back. The former conductor told me that later on after he had been driving for some time, including to London, it became the law that an official inspector had to pass the drivers. (He took the test and needless to say passed it). Mr Sid Ward left the Company during 1951, and sometimes got up a private party of local people and hired a 33-seat coach, which he drove himself, on a private tour. It cost £30 to hire one for the day and he usually charged passengers £1 each, leaving three seats extra, one of these was always a free one for his wife. The afternoon hire usually worked out at about 3/– (15p) each for the passengers. These journeys were well supported, and some people used them in preference to the advertised public tours.

The stage service buses were at this time being driven by Mr Tom Bowden and his son Mr Ernie Bowden as they shared the driving of HYB 676 the AEC Regal, taking turns with each other each day on a shift basis. They had conductresses working with them, one of these being Mrs K Willis who worked with Mr Tom Bowden. JYB 168, the Dennis Lancet, was being regularly driven by Mr Peter Quinn with Mr Fred Passmore as his conductor.

During 1948 GC 4823, an AEC Regal, with Thomas Harrington built 32-seat rear entrance coachwork, arrived from the War Department. It had been new to Messrs Timpsons of Catford during March 1930. It was possibly not licensed to the Minehead company, but there is no confirmation of this and it was disposed of during the same year.

Two Leyland Tiger, type PS1, coaches arrived, one each during March and April 1948, (JYC 855 and

JYC 855, was a Leyland Tiger PS1 with Thomas Harrington 33-seat coachwork, pictured at Weston-super-Mare whilst on a tour to that seaside town.

JYD 199). They were fitted with a Leyland 7.4 litre diesel engine, with 6 cylinders of 4⅜ in bore and 5 in stroke and JYD 199 had been collected by its first regular driver Mr Sid Ward. They had 33-seat well proportioned coachwork by Thomas Harrington. On the front the radiator had a polished chrome surround, which helped to make the appearance more impressive and there was a light blue line along each side surrounded by a narrow polished moulding, which started fairly narrow and widened out a few inches to the end with a small curved piece of moulding to complete it. There were also thin polished metal strips making a moulding around the rear wheels forming a sweeping curve away at the back behind them. There were two more short polished strips enclosed in this, at the rear there was a wide chrome strip, made up of two strips joined together one above the other, which ran along below the luggage compartment doors forming a bumper. The rear number plate was in a recess in this bumper and had a piece of glass in the front of it. Both vehicles were fitted with a dorsal fin, and had two rear glass plates with 'Observation Coach', one word on each plate, painted in blue on a white background. The interior roof was off-white or a very light fawn colour and this was of a material fixed to a solid base making a firm lining. Blue patterned upholstery was used on the seats and also on the side panelling up to window level. Both coaches had individual travelling rugs placed on the back of each seat, for the use of the passengers if

JYD 199, another Leyland Tiger PS1, parked in North Road, Minehead, waiting to operate an afternoon tour. The destination blind is set at 'Lynmouth & Doone Valley'. The photograph was taken on 20 July 1952.

required. These were coloured in shades of blue. Along under the seats near the coach sides there was a copper pipe, which extended down one side, across under the rear seats and back along the opposite side. This was believed to be part of the heating system. Facing the passengers on the front bulkhead there was a clock at the top centre. Each side of this were mirrors with another mirror extending downwards between the windscreen on the left and the window behind the driver's cab. Going across the bulkhead as a dividing line between the windows and the upholstered panelling was pair of polished wood mouldings meeting at the centre. I remember going on a local tour in each of these coaches. Fixed to the bulkhead of JYD 199 was a paper giving the then driver's name (R T Barsby) for these coaches were used on the British Holiday Tours as well as the usual excursions and tours.

By June 1950 Leyland Lion CYB 715 had its original 28-seat pre-war coachwork replaced by new 31-seat coachwork by the original builders, Thomas Harrington. The design of the new coachwork was identical to that of the two Leyland Tigers, except this one was not fitted with a dorsal fin and the pair of rear glass plates were lettered 'Observation Luxury Coach' – the first word was on one plate and the other two on the remaining one. These words were painted in blue on a white background, but on the front glass plate the fleet

43

name was painted in white on a dark blue background. This coach retained its original radiator grille, which was slightly tapered and was bolted in position from a mounting on each side of the radiator surround.

The first new vehicle to be registered to the company during 1950 entered service during May, LYD 581, a Leyland Comet. This was of normal control type with the engine and bonnet projecting out in front with this particular coach having 29-seat coachwork built by Thomas Harrington. There was no destination box fitted – in place of it there were two small windows above the windscreens, each having a curved outer side giving a neatly rounded off appearance. Along above these in the centre was a narrow single glass plate with the fleet name painted in white on a dark blue background. The rear glass plate was lettered 'Luxury Coach'. From the entrance door back the design was the same as that of the larger half cab coaches delivered previously. This coachwork did not have a dorsal fin and the roof was fitted with a sliding panel in the front part, which on fine days could be pulled back opening that part of the roof. The second coach registered during that year was MYA 121, a Leyland Tiger, type PS2, fitted with a Leyland 0/600 (equivalent to 9.8 litre) diesel engine, with 6 cylinders of 4.8 in bore and 5½ in stroke. It was a surprise firstly in that the coachwork was built by H V Burlingham Ltd of Blackpool, and secondly it was built to a full front design seating 33 persons. It was later fitted with a public adddress system so that the driver could speak to the passengers to describe the tours. On the full width front there was a removable panel; attached to this was a row of narrow chrome lines spaced out vertically, the space in between those acted as an air intake for the radiator grille which was concealed behind it. On each side of this panel were some short chrome lines fixed in a horizontal position, these varied in length as did the vertical ones and when looked at all together they formed a half circle. Immediately below the removable panel there was another row of horizontal lines, spaced out to match, on each side of these was a matching fog lamp moulded into the coachwork, these being placed slightly below the main headlamps. There were a pair of narrow chrome strips joined together running right along below, in the position of a bumper. The coach had the usual light blue moulding along each side with a narrow chrome strip fixed around each wheel which swept out well behind it curving back down to the

44

Leyland Lion CYB 715, after being fitted with new 31-seat coachwork by Thomas Harrington. It is seen parked in North Road, Minehead, waiting to operate an afternoon tour to Selworthy and Horner Woods on 20 July 1952.

bottom of the side panelling. Along the bottom of this panelling, between the wheel mouldings, there were three chrome strips. This coach was the heaviest one in the fleet with its unladen weight of 7 tons 2 cwt 0 qrs. It was the only one I can remember which did not have the Blue Motors' oval sign painted on the rear panels. The rear glass plate was lettered 'Luxury Coach' and as on the front glass plate, the writing was in white on a dark blue background. By now the two Albion Victor, type PK 115 coaches. AYC 106 and AYC 107 had been withdrawn from service and sold. The remaining one BYC 341 was sold during the following year, 1951. The last new vehicle registered during 1950 was MYA 246, a second Leyland Comet, this being an identical coach in every respect to the previous one, the coachwork being built by the same coachbuilder. These Comets had

LYD 581, was a Leyland Comet, with 29-seat Thomas Harrington coachwork. It is parked under the branches of a walnut tree at Horner Woods, waiting whilst the passengers have gone for afternon tea. This was on an Over Dunkery Tour on 20 July 1952.

Leyland Tiger PS2, registered MYA 121, had full front 33-seat coachwork built by H V Burlingham. It is seen parked in Summerland Avenue, Minehead.

Leyland P/300, 5.08 litre petrol engines with 6 cylinders of 3.8 in bore and 4½ in stroke.

During 1951 Mr F J Stoate, the Manager and Secretary of the Company for the past thirty years retired. There was a presentation made to him to which every employee subscribed. A gift was also presented to him by the Directors. Mr Stoate was a gentleman held in very high esteem and was well known and respected by many people in the Minehead area. Mr G F R Sandford was subsequently appointed to the position of Manager and Secretary.

About this time the Company started operating some British Holiday Tours, the first known date of departure was September 1951.

During January 1952, the Bedford OWB utility bus GYA 598, was withdrawn and sold. A new Bedford coach was placed in service during February 1952 NYC 993, which was fitted with a Bedford 4.927 litre

MYA 246, was a Leyland Comet and it is seen waiting to operate an afternoon tour to Tarr Steps on 29 June 1952 at North Road, Minehead.

NYC 993, was a Bedford SB having 31-seater Duple coachwork as seen in this view taken at North Road, Minehead. It was waiting to start an afternoon tour on 3 August 1953 and its destination blind is set for 'Lynmouth & Doone Valley'.

petrol engine, with 6 cylinders of 3 in bore and 4¼ in stroke. The coachwork was built by Duple to their Vega design, fitted with a public address system, and having a fairly rounded front with a grille made up of several chrome lines slightly spaced out in a horizontal position. The radiator and engine were placed behind this and above the windscreen on the driver's side there was a glass panel with the fleet name written in copperplate continuous writing, this being painted in dark blue on a white background. Copperplate writing was a new style for the front, but had always been used for the fleet name enclosed inside the oval lines of the Company's sign on the rear panels. Situated in a matching position above the other windscreen was the destination indicator box. Along the sides there was a thin chrome line which started in front of the front wheel then curved upwards straightening out to continue along several inches below the windows, from where it went along the side and then

PYA 973, was a Bedford SB with 33-seat Thomas Harrington coachwork. It is seen waiting in North Road, Minehead, to operate an afternoon tour on 24 September 1953.

curved away downwards to end well behind the rear wheel. There was also a narrow moulding above this one running along with it below the windows only, this was painted light blue. Along the curve of the roof there were quarter lights fitted and inside, the driver was only separated from the passengers by a division which was approximately two feet high from the floor which extended right across the coach behind him, thus giving them a maximum view.

Mr Tom Bowden of Porlock, who had been a driver on the Porlock Weir service for over thirty years retired during February 1952, his last bus being JYB 168, the post war Dennis Lancet. He was presented with a watch from the Company, and also a collection (to which about 250 people subscribed) was made for him in the Porlock area, in appreciation of his services to them. A radio set was presented to him at the Methodist Church, Porlock, of which he was a member.

During the summer of 1952, the first Leyland Cheetah DYC 20, was noted operating as a duplicate on the stage service.

One of the worst disasters ever to happen in the area occurred during the nights of Friday and Saturday, 15/16 August 1952 – the dreadful flooding at Lynmouth. After torrential rain, water had built up higher in the valley of the Lyn rivers, which was released during the night and with such awful force that the water hit buildings, demolishing some and damaging others. The town was completely devastated and much of it, including the old harbour wall, was washed away. At the time, in addition to the local people, the town had many people staying there on holiday. The following day, the Saturday, during the emergency situation there, the local bus and coach operators of Minehead and their staff, did a great deal to help. About 600 local residents (many homeless) and holiday makers were taken to a reception centre at Minehead, or direct to the railway station to return home.

I quote from the *West Somerset Free Press* newspaper of 23 August 1952:

Fine Transport Achievement, twenty-one journeys:–
    In response to a request from the Police in the morning Mr F J Holman, Minehead depot, Western National Omnibus Company, put arrangements immediately in hand in conjunction with the manager of Blue Motors (Mr G F R Sandford), and Messrs Hawkins Bros (Scarlet Pimpernel Coaches), for bringing in the evacuated people.

In all during the day twenty-one journeys were run, of which Blue Motors and Scarlet Pimpernel shared half a dozen between them. The Western National also ran four coaches to Lynton, via the Barnstaple route, that day, with evacuated Lynmouth residents. This was done at the request of the Lynton and Lynmouth UDC. The vehicles going on the Lynmouth journey could go no further down Countisbury Hill than the widened part near the Beacon Hotel, and evacuees, except for those who walked up, were taken up to the coaches in police cars and Army lorries.

Also from *The Busmen's Share*:

A feeder service was set up to bring people up from Lynmouth Hill, and the supply of vehicles at Lynton, as time went on, was augmented by Blue Motors. More buses were sent from Ilfracombe by Mr E A Venables (Traffic Superintendent), who displayed a quick appreciation of the position. Hundreds of people were conveyed to Barnstaple – 500 on Saturday morning alone – and everything was handled with expedition. Every post since then has contained letters of appreciation of the courtesy and efficiency displayed by Inspector Sutton, and the bus drivers and conductors.

The Western National Company, the Blue Motors Company, and Messrs Hawkins Bros, didn't make any charge to the authorities for their coaches used in the evacuation to Minehead. Many of the staff who took part gave their services free for the extra work required of them.

It was during February 1953 that two of the Leyland Cheetahs, DYC 20 and EYB 488 were withdrawn from service and sold. A new Bedford SB coach was collected from the coachbuilders at Hove by Mr Eric Tarr, its driver, who had previously been the driver in charge of EYB 488. The new coach was PYA 973, having 33-seat coachwork built by Thomas Harrington, and was the first eight foot wide coach to be operated from Minehead. On each side of the windscreen there were windows which curved around with the corner of the coachwork matching up with the windows along the sides. Above each windscreen there was a small window making a matching pair, these having a curved outer side neatly rounding off the appearance. Placed along above these in the centre there was a single narrow glass plate with the Blue Motors' name on it in capital letters, these being painted in white on a dark blue background. The grille was made up of a variety of horizontal chrome lines

PYB 383, another Bedford SB, with Duple Coachwork, built to the Super Vega Coronation design, seating 35 passengers. It is seen parked in Summerland Avenue, Minehead.

and on the sides there was a thin chrome line which started in front of the front wheel, then curved around over the top of it from where it continued across the side panel going downwards to end near the bottom of the panelling just in front of the rear wheel. From here there was another thin chrome line which followed around the rear wheel curving out around it in a sweep to end at the bottom of the panelling towards the back. Along the side a few inches below the windows there was a single chrome line about two inches wide which swept slightly downwards towards the rear of the coach. The rear glass plate was lettered 'Luxury Coach'.

During June 1953 another Bedford SB coach was registered, PYB 383, which had Duple built coachwork seating 35 passengers. It was of a similar design to the Vega style fitted on the 1952 coach, but this one being of the later Super Vega Coronation pattern. The main difference was at the front, where this one had windscreens which curved away with a considerable sweep along the lower edge from the centre pillar towards the opposite corners. Above each windscreen on the curve of the roof there was a half light fitted, these appeared to be tinted orange in colour. The grille was also different, being much more elaborate, and under

50

A view taken at Porlock Weir during the 1930s showing left to right: Conductor, Mr Francis Freegard; Driver, Dick Boyle, a young visitor to the area; and Conductor Mr Sid Ward. The buses are, in the background: a Dennis Lancet, by the rear entrance it would be YD 4593, and YC 599 an Albion with Duple bodywork (after its seating capacity had been reduced to 26 passengers).

the chrome makers' nameplate there was a wide chrome strip with slits in it. Below this was a row of horizontal chrome lines of varying lengths, and running vertical down the centre of these was a narrow moulding with what appears to be a white coloured panel fitted. On each side of the grille, fairly low down, there was a small chrome pressing with slits in it. On the side panels the lines were as on the 1952 coach, the only exception being the moulding along under the windows for this one had a chrome line in it instead of being painted. There were quarter lights fitted along the curve of the roof on each side and the rear glass plate was lettered 'Luxury Coach'. The last two Bedford SBs would have had the same type of engine as the first one, NYC 993. They each had a public address system fitted.

The bus service was sold to the Western National Omnibus Co Ltd during June 1953, along with the two service buses HYB 676 and JYB 168 and some of the staff were transferred to Western National, including driver Mr Ernie Bowden.

During April 1954 the Company amalgamated with Messrs Hawkins Bros, 'Scarlet Pimpernel Coaches' of Minehead, to form a new Company, 'Scarlet and Blue Motor Coaches Ltd', and the remaining coaches (which

51

continued to be operated in their Blue Motors' livery for several years after, with those of the Scarlet Pimpernel fleet which retained their scarlet red livery) were transferred to the new Company.

It is interesting to note that during the early 1960s the Porlock Weir stage carriage service was back in independent operation by the direct descendant of the Blue Motors, and of the Scarlet and Blue Motor Coaches Ltd, the 'Scarlet Coaches, Minehead', owned by Mr D C Venner who had bought the firm during the 1960s.

3

Operating the bus service

The bus service departure place was from the Railway Station approach at Minehead where the waiting passenger would see the Blue Motors' dark blue bus turn in the Railway Station yard, go down towards the end then turn around in a circle and come up to a halt at the bus stop. This was alongside a hedge of a nearby hotel, on the opposite side of the approach from the railway station buildings. The railway line continues a short way on the end right up to the road which runs along the Esplanade. We board the bus, on this occasion HYB 676, an AEC Regal with Thomas Harrington 35-seat bodywork, and take our seat about halfway down the bus. From the bus one gets a fine view, by looking over the sea front which curves around the bay. In front of us one can see the Bristol Channel and beyond this, on a clear day, the Welsh coast is visible in the distance. Looking slightly to the left near the end of the Esplanade one can see the North Hill which, after running along behind the town, comes down steeply to near the Quay and harbour wall.

The driver climbs into his cab, shuts his door and starts the engine. The conductor boards the bus and slides the door shut. He is wearing a soft cover peaked cap and a grey overall coat, with the money bag and Williamson ticket punch straps across each other over it. He goes down the bus collecting the fares and issuing the tickets from a two-tier ticket rack. We hear the 'ting' of the ticket punch as he cancels them. We set off turning immediately to our left into The Avenue, where we continue along past the shops and the Company's office on our right. A stop is made at the bus stop outside the Western National Company office and depot. We go on through the main part of the town, where there are most of the shops with the market over to our right, The Avenue now goes into the Square which is our next stop. Here there is a fine statue of Queen Anne. We pull away on past more shops and the Post Office; bearing right we continue on past houses then curve around to the left. This is a residential area called 'The Parks'.

Our next stop is at the top of Woodcombe Lane which

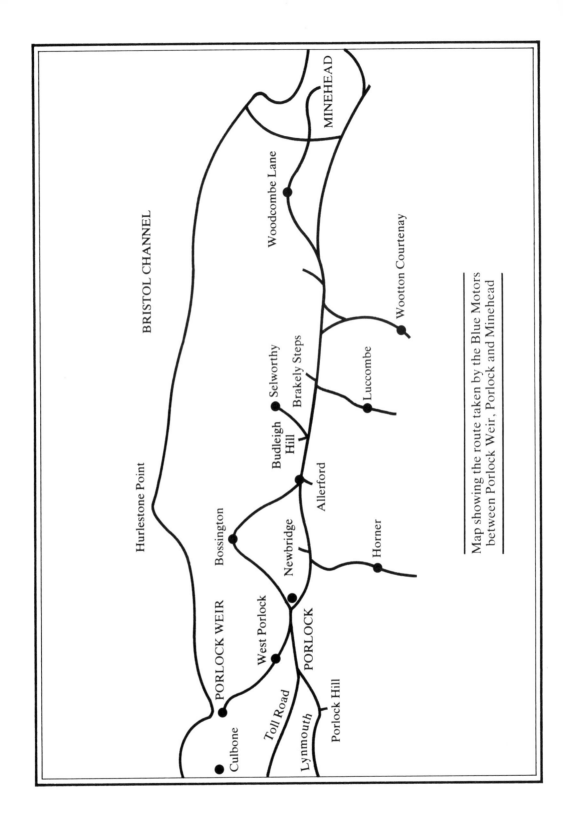

Map showing the route taken by the Blue Motors between Porlock Weir, Porlock and Minehead

goes off on our right and we are now out in the country. After bearing around left we continue on past the Cemetery on our left to the junction of the main road, the A39, which by-passes and runs along behind the town from Alcombe. Here we turn right pulling away along a very attractive wide valley. On the left we have a hill rising up away from us. On our right some way over is another hill, this one is very high and runs along for some miles. On past the narrow turning to Bratton on our right, which falls away steeply from the main road and on down over a fairly long hill where we are gradually curving away to our right. Then we go along more straight road, up over a slight hill, then on our left we pass the first turning to Wooton Courtenay. Then on to stop at a second turning to this village and Timberscombe. We set off again along the now fairly winding road which rises and falls frequently. The next stop is called Brakeley Steps, this is at the turning off on our left to Luccombe, a picturesque village situated some way over from the main road. Off again, along this road there is always the odd cottage or two spaced well out, as we go to Budleigh Hill, this is the stop for Selworthy, which is away on our right. To get there one has to walk down a lane almost covered right over by the overhanging branches of the trees from both sides. The village is one of the most picturesque in the area, many of the cottages having thatched roofs. The Church with its short tower, being coloured white, shows up well on the hillside above the village. This is very much one of the Olde-Worlde villages we hear about in this area and is owned by The National Trust. The hill continues along high up behind the village and as with the other hills in the district, this one is covered with purple-coloured heather, which when it is in flower during the late summer, makes a striking background.

We start off again along the main road. Near here on our left is Holnicot House, formerly the home of Sir Richard Acland who gave his estate, which included Selworthy and Bossington, to the National Trust. On we go, the road winds about also narrowing in places until we come to Brandish Street, (called Brandy Street by Mrs Willis), this being a group of houses mainly on our right, which are joined on to Allerford where we now are. It is a very old village; from here there is a lane which turns off to the right, this goes to Bossington and some journeys operate via this route, but these are few and I will deal with these later on. Again we have an assortment of picturesque thatched cottages. On bearing around left then right, we go on over a small stone bridge, with a stream under it, and further on we stop next at Newbridge. From here a lane goes off to our right through a valley in the hills. This leads to Horner Woods where there is a hamlet with several cottages, these being situated at the foot of Dunkery Beacon, the highest point on Exmoor which rises up behind. There is a small green and a stream which flows through the woods runing near the roadside, with an old mill and waterwheel which has long ceased to turn. There are several walnut trees near the green.

Back on the main road at Newbridge we keep travelling on in the comfortable bus, with its engine purring away. Up front we can see the back of our driver in the half cab, whilst our conductor is standing ready for the next passengers to board us. He has to slide the entrance door open for boarding passengers, then close it for them. We continue on until we go down over a short steep hill at the bottom of which we curve around left towards the village of Porlock. At this point we join the lane from Bossington, going back to Allerford. The journeys which operate via Bossington turn off right from the main road, on around a bend past the famous pack horse bridge on our right (this has been photographed many times and the picture used for greeting cards), continuing on down the lane which is very narrow we mostly have a stream on our right. On past the old thatched school on our right whilst rising away on this side high above is Bossington Beacon and Hurlestone Point. Again in summertime these are covered with areas of ferns and heather. Next are some cottages as we enter the village of Bossington with yet more cottages on both sides, keeping left at the village green which is the bus stop. Another lane goes off along the right-hand side of it, the stream we had seen went away right through the woods at the foot of the beacon.

We set off along a narrow lane curving away to the left and from here one can look over to the right across level land to the pebble ridge behind which is the sea. On along the lane past some cottages on both sides of us until we go under some overhanging trees and down over a steep hill. At the foot of this we join the road from Newbridge. This hill is a triangle and the traffic operates on a keep left system, incoming traffic from Newbridge comes down one side and traffic from Bossington comes down the other side, outgoing traffic keeps left up over a steep hill on the Bossington side. Traffic for Bossington keeps straight on and traffic to Minehead turns very sharp right near the top of the hill making a hairpin bend, then continuing up another immediate climb then it joins the incoming road from Newbridge. I recollect making a journey from Porlock Weir to Minehead during the summer months about 1950, two buses being used to operate the journey. I was travelling in the first one, and as we went up the first part of the hill, around the hairpin bend and started climbing the second part, I well remember looking downwards out of the window and onto the dark blue roof of the second bus which was climbing the first part of the hill immediately below us.

Returning now past the War Memorial on our right at the foot of the hill, we start to enter the fairly large village of Porlock with its cottages, houses and some shops on both sides of the narrow streets, so we go on with some caution. During the summer months there are often quite a lot of tourists in the village. We pass the Parish Church on our left with the top of its spire missing and as we pass through, various stops are made to set down and pick up passengers. Around to the right and on past the Central Garage on our right; this is a general garage and outside of their office we can distinguish some Blue Motors' excursions and tours advertisement boards displayed, for this being the Company's Booking Agent at Porlock. Shortly after the main road branches away from us on our left, at the road on to Lynmouth and nearby is the famous Porlock Hill which is 1 in 4 steep. One can also, as an alternative, use the toll road which forks off right shortly before the bottom of the hill. We continue straight ahead past a few more houses then into the country again.

We are now going along with the wooded slopes towering above us on our left, the ground being level on the opposite side across to the sea. We pass a few cottages and houses as we bear around to the right. This is West Porlock, but there is no mention of it by name on the timetables. We carry on straight for a while then we bear around right, on past the Blue Motors' garage on our right. Bearing around left we continue along with a wall by us on our right, behind this is a pebble beach leading down to the sea. On our left-hand side we pass some cottages, near the Ship Inn. All along behind these are the tree-covered slopes of the hill which climbs high above us for this is Porlock Weir. The road comes to an end in front of the Anchor Hotel, the bus stops, then backs around where a small lane goes off, straightening up. The bus then drives forward across the road to stop alongside a low wall by the car park for this is our stop, where the driver can switch off the engine whilst the bus waits for some minutes before departing on the return journey to Minehead.

Porlock Weir is a very attractive place. If one walks on past the Anchor Hotel there are more cottages and a shop. The harbour comes in around here and there are usually a few boats and yachts moored. The path ends high up at the water's edge, but there is a bridge with iron handrails which spans the entrance to the inner harbour and when a ship goes through this bridge, it is pulled back on small rollers sunk into the path behind it. After going across the bridge one can walk around a very substantial stone harbour wall which separates the harbour from the sea. From the end of the wall one can look across the Bristol Channel, or along the beach on the opposite side of the harbour; one can follow this around to the large hill in the distance which is jutting out into the sea – this is Hurlestone Point. Looking away in the opposite direction from the wall there is the small inner harbour, which is sometimes used by ships to unload coal into lorries which are backed onto the edge of this harbour. The pebble beach with the hills rising almost sheer follow on behind it curving away out of sight towards Lynmouth. From the wall one can have a fine view by looking across the harbour of the whole of Porlock Weir. Just inside of the wall near where the bus is waiting is a large car park. After waiting its allowed time the bus sets off back to Minehead.

The journey time for a direct journey is 35 minutes each way, and for a journey via Bossington the time taken is 40 minutes each way. Two different timetables were printed during the year, one for the summer months which during 1934 had fourteen journeys to Porlock Weir and thirteen journeys to Minehead on weekdays and ten journeys each way on Sundays (this being when the Blue Motors operated separate to the Western National Omnibus Company). Later on after the joint operation was in force there were during 1951 and 1952 thirty-six journeys each way on weekdays and eighteen journeys each way on Sundays. This latter timetable was in operation between June and September, the other timetable for the winter months which during 1949, 1951 and 1952 had eleven journeys each way on weekdays and six journeys each way on

Karrier Y 4265. This was the service bus used mostly on the service route during much of the 1920s. The man standing by it was the Manager, Mr Tom Priscott. (Note the radiator top is painted.) c. 1920.

Sundays. Each of the two operators shared the journeys between them. Along the route the Blue Motors had their own fairly large timetable boards, with their own printed timetable displayed on them. These were at many of the bus stops and were often placed next to the Western National timetable boards. These would have dated from when the two companies operated separate to each other. Some timetables made mention of 'Parcels taken at owner's risk', additionally that return tickets issued on Blue Motors' vehicles could be utilised for the return journey on Western National vehicles and vice versa.

There were duplicate vehicles used on some journeys, especially during the summer months, pre-war, when there was a duplicate bus or buses used for a journey. One conductor was usually in charge, at Minehead Railway Station. He would collect the fares on the duplicate bus or buses first, then they would start off ahead to set down passengers only, he would then board the actual service operating bus, and ride on it collecting the fares as usual. Sometimes he would ride on one bus collecting the fares as it went along The Avenue, then leave it at The Square to go on ahead. He would then board the next one there and collect the fares on that.

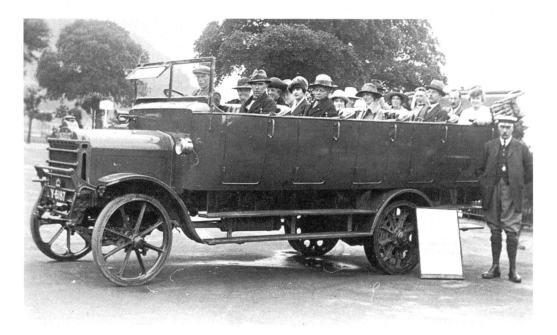

Daimler char-a-banc Y 6187, with bodywork built by A G Dowell of Exeter. It is seen parked at Minehead Railway Station approach during 1920, waiting to start for Porlock Weir. (Note its solid tyres, also the timetable board.) The driver is a young Mr Charlie Babb.

Sometimes a duplicate bus would run to Budleigh Hill, Selworthy turn, then return to Minehead, and when busy would set off for there again.

On some journeys it happened that a bus was full up on leaving Minehead, however most of the passengers were 1d or 2d fares to Woodcombe and this was only a short way out, so after setting these down the bus would go on nearly empty.

I well remember several occasions when two vehicles were used together (sometimes more) to operate one journey at a time, but this became rare by 1950.

The vehicles used to operate the service journeys over the years were as follows:

1916 to 1927: Y 4265, the Karrier 35-seat bus, which was helped out when necessary with char-a-bancs; the Daimler Y 6187 was known to have been used some time during 1920, also the Crossleys were used, using which one was available at the time.

1927 to 1932: YC 599, the Albion PK 26, Duple 29-seat bus, was the main one used, and from 1929 YC 7355, a Dennis with 20 seats was used as well as a one-man operated vehicle. The two Albion PN 26, 'Open' 26-seat coaches, YB 5914 and YB 5915 were used sometimes to help out.

1932/4 to 1940: YD 4593 and YD 9697, both Dennis Lancet 1s, with Duple 32-seat bodywork were used as a pair, with the Albion bus YC 599, now seating 26, being used as a duplicate when needed.

Conductress Miss Sybil Wood, seen wearing the white with blue relief dress and bag her mother made for her. With her is driver Mr Bill Manley. The coach CYB 715 is a Leyland Lion with its first coachwork and is seen with a war-time shade over the headlamp along with a white flash on the mudguard.

1940 to 1946: the remaining coaches including CYB 715, Leyland Lion with its 28-seat Thomas Harrington coachwork, and the Leyland Cheetahs were used. From 1945 Bedford OWB, Duple, 32-seat utility bus, GYA 598, came into service.

1946/7 to 1953: AEC Regal HYB 676 and JYB 168, the Dennis Lancet J3, both with 35-seat Thomas Harrington bodywork were used as a pair, with coaches helping out; AYC 106 and AYC 107, both Albion Victor, Thomas Harrington 26-seat coaches were used with GYA 598 Bedford utility bus to work with HYB 676 during the summer about 1947. This utility bus was used as duplicate until the end of 1951, then for the summer of 1952 DYC 20, Leyland Cheetah, Thomas Harrington 27-seat coach was used as the duplicate, being driven by its regular coach driver Mr J H Day.

The company always had bus drivers and coach drivers. Normally they kept to their respective duties,

A view looking up The Avenue at Minehead, with a Blue Motors' bus stopped near the Parade. It would be either HYB 676 or JYB 168.

Left to right: Drivers – Mr Dick Boyle and Mr Bill Manley, along with Mildred Rayment; Conductors – Mr Sid Ward and Mr Ernie Bowden, stood in front of Dennis Lancet YD 4593 during August 1938.

Back row, left to right: Drivers – Mr Tom Bowden and Mr Peter Quinn; Conductress – Miss Rita Middleton and Driver Mr Charlie Headford. In front Mr Charlie Babb and Driver Mr Bill Manley.

but sometimes coach drivers helped out by driving a service bus on service journeys. Mr Eric Tarr helped out sometimes by driving JYB 168 on the service route during a winter, but usually the service buses each had their own driver who kept to them on service timings.

For further recollections of the bus services journeys, attention is drawn to the book *Memoirs of Selworthy and West Somerset* by Cicely Elaine Cooper, published by Cox, Sons and Co Ltd, Williton, Somerset (first edition 1951, second edition 1966), in which there is a chapter entitled 'The Blue Motors', telling of her experiences of the Porlock Weir-Minehead service.

Timetables

The above print is of the timetable which stood by the Daimler char-a-banc, shown previously. The original photograph was taken during 1920. Departure times from Minehead were: 10.35 am, 1.20, 2.55 and 6.15 pm. The vehicle kept to the main road and passengers for the places named on the timetable had to alight at the same stopping places for them as in later years. Then they had to walk to the villages of either Selworthy or Horner Woods. There is mention on the timetable of giving time at Porlock Weir to visit Culbone Church, which meant that the vehicle would wait at Porlock Weir long enough for people to walk through the woods to visit Culbone Church (this is said to be the smallest Parish Church in England, still in regular use for worship) and back again.

Porlock We_r, _orlock & Minehead Motor Serv_ce _ompany, Limited.

Registered Offices—25, The Avenue, Minehead. Telephone 75.

BLUE MOTORS.

Daily Motor Service
BETWEEN
Minehead and Porlock Weir

Including all Places of Interest en Route, from July 9th, 1934, until further notice

TIME TABLE.

WEEK-DAYS.

	A.M.	A.M.	A.M.	P.M.	P.M.	P.M.	P.M.	P.M.	P.M.	P.M.	P.M.	P.M.	P.M.	P.M. T.
MINEHEAD STATION .... dep.	9.30	10.30	11.30	12.30	1.30	2.30	3.30	4.30	5.30	6.30	7.30	8.30	9.40	10.15
MINEHEAD SQUARE	9.33	10.33	11.33	12.33	1.33	2.33	3.33	4.33	5.33	6.33	7.33	8.33	9.43	10.18
BRAKELEY STEPS (for Luccombe)...	9.44	10.44	11.44	12.44	1.44	2.44	3.44	4.44	5.44	6.44	7.44	8.44	9.54	10.29
BUDLEIGH HILL (for Selworthy)..	9.47	10.47	11.47	12.47	1.47	2.47	3.47	4.47	5.47	6.47	7.47	8.47	9.57	10.32
ALLERFORD	9.50	10.50	11.50	12.50	1.50	2.50	3.50	4.50	5.50	6.50	7.50	8.50	10.0	10.35
BOSSINGTON GREEN	—	—	—	—	1.55	—	—	4.55	—	—	—	—	—	—
NEWBRIDGE (for Horner)	9.53	10.53	11.53	12.53	—	2.53	3.53	—	5.53	6.53	7.53	8.53	10.3	10.38
PORLOCK	9.58	10.58	11.58	12.58	2.3	2.58	3.58	5.3	5.58	6.58	7.58	8.58	10.8	10.43
PORLOCK WEIR .... arr.	10.5	11.5	12.5	1.5	2.10	3.5	4.5	5.20	6.5	7.5	8.5	9.5	10.15	10.50

T Wednesdays, Thursdays, and Saturdays. This Bus waits until close of performance at Theatre.

	A.M.	A.M.	A.M.	A.M.	P.M.	P.M.	P.M.	P.M.	P.M.	P.M.	P.M.	P.M.	P.M.
PORLOCK WEIR .... dep.	8.20	9.15	10.15	11.15	12.15	1.15	2.15	3.15	4.15	5.15	6.15	7.15	8.15
PORLOCK	8.30	9.25	10.25	11.25	12.25	1.25	2.25	3.25	4.25	5.25	6.25	7.25	8.25
NEWBRIDGE	—	9.28	10.28	11.28	12.28	1.28	—	3.28	4.28	5.28	6.28	7.28	8.28
BOSSINGTON GREEN	8.35	—	—	—	—	—	2.30	—	—	—	—	—	—
ALLERFORD	8.40	9.31	10.31	11.31	12.31	1.31	2.35	3.31	4.31	5.31	6.31	7.31	8.31
BUDLEIGH HILL	8.43	9.34	10.34	11.34	12.34	1.34	2.38	3.34	4.34	5.34	6.34	7.34	8.34
BRAKELEY STEPS	8.46	9.37	10.37	11.37	12.37	1.37	2.41	3.37	4.37	5.37	6.37	7.37	8.37
MINEHEAD SQUARE	8.57	9.48	10.48	11.48	12.48	1.48	2.52	3.48	4.48	5.48	6.48	7.48	8.48
MINEHEAD STATION .... arr.	9.0	9.50	10.50	11.50	12.50	1.50	2.55	3.50	4.50	5.50	6.50	7.50	8.50

SUNDAYS.

	A.M.	P.M.	P.M.	P.M.	P.M.	P.M.	P.M.	P.M.	P.M.	P.M.
MINEHEAD STATION .... dep.	10.0	12.20	2.30	3.30	4.30	5.30	6.30	7.30	8.30	9.30
MINEHEAD SQUARE	10.3	12.22	2.33	3.33	4.33	5.33	6.33	7.33	8.33	9.33
BRAKELEY STEPS (for Luccombe)...	10.14	12.34	2.44	3.44	4.44	5.44	6.44	7.44	8.44	9.44
BUDLEIGH HILL (for Selworthy)...	10.17	12.37	2.47	3.47	4.47	5.47	6.47	7.47	8.47	9.47
ALLERFORD	10.20	12.40	2.50	3.50	4.50	5.50	6.50	7.50	8.50	9.50
NEWBRIDGE (for Horner)	10.23	12.43	2.53	3.53	4.53	5.53	6.53	7.53	8.53	9.53
PORLOCK	10.28	12.48	2.58	3.58	4.58	5.58	6.58	7.58	8.58	9.58
PORLOCK WEIR .... arr.	10.35	12.55	3.5	4.5	5.5	6.5	7.5	8.5	9.5	10.5

	A.M.	P.M.	P.M.	P.M.	P.M.	P.M.	P.M.	P.M.	P.M.	P.M.
PORLOCK WEIR .... dep.	10.15	12.15	2.15	3.15	4.15	5.15	6.15	7.15	8.15	9.15
PORLOCK	10.25	12.25	2.25	3.25	4.25	5.25	6.25	7.25	8.25	9.25
NEWBRIDGE	10.28	12.28	2.28	3.28	4.28	5.28	6.28	7.28	8.28	9.28
ALLERFORD	10.31	12.31	2.31	3.31	4.31	5.31	6.31	7.31	8.31	9.31
BUDLEIGH HILL	10.34	12.34	2.34	3.34	4.34	5.34	6.34	7.34	8.34	9.34
BRAKELEY STEPS	10.37	12.37	2.37	3.37	4.37	5.37	6.37	7.37	8.37	9.37
MINEHEAD SQUARE	10.48	12.48	2.48	3.48	4.48	5.48	6.48	7.48	8.48	9.48
MINEHEAD STATION .... arr.	10.50	12.50	2.50	3.50	4.50	5.50	6.50	7.50	8.50	9.50

FARES.

MINEHEAD to

		SINGLE.	RETURN.
Porlock Weir }			
Mariner's Combe } ...	...	9d.	1/3
Porlock Ford ... }			
West Porlock ...	...	8d.	1/2
Porlock	...	7d.	1/0
Allerford and Newbridge	...	6d.	10d.
Budleigh Hill	...	5d.	9d.
Brakeley Steps	...	4d.	8d.
Venniford Cross and Box	...	3d.	6d.
Bratton Wall	...	3d.	
Middlecombe (from Station) 3d.		(from Town)	2d.
Cemetery	...	2d.	
Woodcombe (from Station) 2d.		(from Town)	1d.

Unemployed (Fridays) 8d. Return.

PORLOCK WEIR to

				SINGLE.	RETURN.
Porlock ...	...	...	...	2d.	3d.
Allerford ...	...	...	...	4d.	8d.
Budleigh Hill	...	...	...	5d.	9d.
Brakeley Steps	...	...	...	6d.	10d.
Bratton Wall	...	...	...	7d.	1/-

PORLOCK to

			SINGLE.	RETURN.
Allerford ...	...	...	2d.	4d.
Budleigh Hill	...	...	3d.	6d.
Brakeley Steps	...	...	4d.	8d.

PICTURE BUS. Available only on Buses departing from Porlock Weir between 5.30 p.m. and 7.15 p.m.

Porlock Weir to Minehead	...	10d. (Return).	
Porlock	...	9d.	„
Allerford and Budleigh Hill	...	7d.	„

PASSENGERS LUGGAGE CONVEYED. For any other information apply to the Company's Servants.

PARCELS TAKEN AT OWNER'S RISK.

The Company will not be responsible for any delay in connection with this Service.
ALL COMMUNICATIONS TO BE ADDRESSED TO THE MANAGER, BLUE MOTORS.

Private Cars for Hire.

The Blue Motors timetable for 1934.

PORLOCK WEIR, PORLOCK AND MINEHEAD MOTOR SERVICE CO., LTD.

Registered Offices :—39, The Avenue, Minehead.

Telephone 75.

BLUE MOTORS

Daily Motor Service between Minehead and Porlock Weir

TIME TABLE

Joint Service with the Western National Omnibus Company, Ltd.

WEEK DAYS

FROM 24th SEPTEMBER, 1951, UNTIL FURTHER NOTICE.

	A.M.	A.M.	A.M.	A.M. (B)	P.M.	P.M.	P.M. (B)	P.M.	P.M.	P.M. (B)	P.M. (W.S.)
Minehead Station] *dep.*	7.30	8.48	10. 0	11.45	1.10	2.10	4.15	5.36	6.53	9.15	10.35
Minehead W.N. Office or Square	7.31	8.49	10. 1	11.46	1.11	2.11	4.16	5.37	6.54	9.16	10.36
Woodcombe Lane	7.35	8.53	10. 5	11.50	1.15	2.15	4.20	5.41	6.58	9.20	10.40
Brakeley Steps	7.43	9. 1	10.13	11.58	1.23	2.23	4.28	5.49	7. 6	9.28	10.48
Budleigh Hill (*for Selworthy*)	7.46	9. 4	10.16	12. 1	1.26	2.26	4.31	5.52	7. 9	9.31	10.51
Allerford	7.49	9. 7	10.19	12. 4	1.29	2.29	4.34	5.55	7.12	9.34	10.54
Bossington Green				12. 9			4.39			9.39	
Newbridge	7.52	9.10	10.22		1.32	2.32		5.58	7.15		10.57
Porlock	7.55	9.13	10.25	12.15	1.35	2.35	4.45	6. 1	7.18	9.45	11. 0
Porlock Weir *arr.*	8. 5	9.23	10.35	12.25	1.45	2.45	4.55	6.11	7.28	9.55	11.10

	A.M.	A.M.	A.M.	A.M. (B)	P.M.	P.M.	P.M. (B)	P.M.	P.M.	P.M. (B)	P.M. (W.S.)
Porlock Weir *dep.*	8. 7	9.24	10.36	12.30	1.50	2.50	5. 0	6.12	7.30	9.57	11.11
Porlock	8.17	9.34	10.46	12.40	2. 0	3. 0	5.10	6.22	7.40	10. 7	11.21
Newbridge		9.37	10.49	12.43		3. 3	5.13		7.43	10.10	11.24
Bossington Green	8.23				2. 6			6.28			
Allerford	8.28	9.40	10.52	12.46	2.11	3. 6	5.16	6.33	7.46	10.13	11.27
Budleigh Hill (*for Selworthy*)	8.31	9.43	10.55	12.49	2.14	3. 9	5.19	6.36	7.49	10.16	11.30
Brakeley Steps	8.34	9.46	10.58	12.52	2.17	3.12	5.22	6.39	7.52	10.19	11.33
Woodcombe Lane	8.42	9.54	11. 6	1. 0	2.25	3.20	5.30	6.47	8. 0	10.27	11.41
Minehead Square	8.45	9.57	11. 9	1. 3	2.28	3.23	5.33	6.50	8. 3	10.30	11.44
Minehead Station *arr.*	8.47	9.59	11.11	1. 5	2.30	3.25	5.35	6.52	8. 5	10.32	

B—Via Bossington.   W.S.—Wednesdays and Saturdays only.

SUNDAYS

FROM 23rd SEPTEMBER, 1951, UNTIL FURTHER NOTICE.

	A.M.	P.M.	P.M.	P.M. (B)	P.M.	P.M.	P.M.
Minehead Station *dep.*	9.15	12.15	1.35	4.10	5.35		8.25
Minehead W.N. Office or Square	9.16	12.16	1.36	4.11	5.36		8.26
Woodcombe Lane	9.20	12.20	1.40	4.15	5.40		8.30
Brakeley Steps	9.28	12.28	1.48	4.23	5.48		8.38
Budleigh Hill (*for Selworthy*)	9.31	12.31	1.51	4.26	5.51		8.41
Allerford	9.34	12.34	1.54	4.29	5.54		8.44
Bossington Green					5.59		
Newbridge	9.37	12.37	1.57	4.32			8.47
Porlock	9.40	12.40	2. 0	4.35	6. 5		8.50
Porlock Weir *arr.*	9.50	12.50	2.10	4.45	6.15		9. 0

	A.M.	P.M.	P.M. (B)	P.M.	P.M.	P.M.
Porlock Weir *dep.*	9.55	12.55	2.15	4.50	6.20	9. 5
Porlock	10. 5	1. 5	2.25	5. 0	6.30	9.15
Newbridge	10. 8	1. 8		5. 3	6.33	9.18
Bossington Green			2.31			
Allerford	10.11	1.11	2.36	5. 6	6.36	9.21
Budleigh Hill (*for Selworthy*)	10.14	1.14	2.39	5. 9	6.39	9.24
Brakeley Steps	10.17	1.17	2.42	5.12	6.42	9.27
Woodcombe Lane	10.25	1.25	2.50	5.20	6.50	9.35
Minehead Square	10.28	1.28	2.53	5.23	6.53	9.38
Minehead Station *arr.*	10.30	1.30	2.55	5.25	6.55	9.40

B—Via Bossington.

Parcels taken at Owner's risk.   The Company will not be responsible for any delay in connection with this Service.

All communications to be addressed to the Manager, Blue Motors.

Cox, Printers, Minehead.

The timetable for 1951.

PORLOCK WEIR, PORLOCK AND MINEHEAD MOTOR SERVICE CO., LTD.

Registered Offices :—39, The Avenue, Minehead.   TELEPHONE 75.

BLUE MOTORS

DAILY MOTOR SERVICE BETWEEN MINEHEAD AND PORLOCK WEIR

SUMMER TIME TABLE

JOINT SERVICE WITH THE WESTERN NATIONAL OMNIBUS CO. LTD.

Return Tickets issued on Blue Motor Vehicles may be utilised for the return journey on Western National vehicles and vice versa.

Week-Days

16th JUNE to 20th SEPTEMBER, 1952, inclusive.

	am	am	am	am	am	am	am	am	am	am	pm	pm	pm	pm	pm	pm	pm	pm
Minehead (Railway Station) dep.	7.30	8.46	9.20	9.45	10.5	10.22	10.45	11.5	11.25	11.42	12.5	12.25	12.45	1.5	1.25	1.45	2.5	2.25
Minehead (W. N Office or Square)	7.31	8.49	9.21	9.46	10.6	10.23	10.46	11.6	11.26	11.43	12.6	12.26	12.46	1.6	1.26	1.46	2.6	2.26
Woodcombe Lane	7.35	8.53	9.25	9.50	10.10	10.27	10.50	11.10	11.30	11.47	12.10	12.30	12.50	1.10	1.30	1.50	2.10	2.30
Brakeley Steps	7.43	9.1	9.33	9.58	10.12	10.35	10.58	11.18	11.38	11.55	12.18	12.38	12.58	1.18	1.38	1.58	2.18	2.31
Budleigh Hill (for Selworthy)	7.46	9.4	9.36	10.1	10.21	10.38	11.1	11.21	11.41	11.58	12.21	12.41	1.1	1.21	1.41	2.1	2.21	2.41
Allerford	7.49	9.7	9.39	10.4	10.24	10.41	11.4	11.24	11.44	12.1	12.24	12.44	1.4	1.24	1.44	2.4	2.24	2.44
Bossington (Green)						10.16				12.6								
Newbridge	7.52	9.10	9.42	10.7	10.27		11.7	11.27	11.47		12.27	12.47	1.7	1.27	1.47	2.7	2.27	2.47
Porlock	7.55	9.13	9.46	10.10	10.30	10.52	11.10	11.30	11.50	12.12	12.30	12.50	1.10	1.30	1.50	2.10	2.30	2.50
Porlock Weir arr.	8.5	9.24	9.55	10.20	10.40	11.2	11.20	11.40	12.0	12.22	12.40	1.0	1.20	1.40	2.0	2.20	2.40	3.0

	pm	pm	pm	pm	pm	pm	pm	pm	pm	pm	pm	pm	pm	pm	pm	pm	pm	pm
Minehead (Railway Station) dep.	2.45	3.2	3.25	3.45	4.5	4.22	4.45	5.5	5.25	5.46	6.5	6.25	7.5	7.46	8.25	9.5	9.42	10.25
Minehead (W. N Office or Square)	2.46	3.3	3.26	3.46	4.6	4.23	4.46	5.6	5.26	5.46	6.6	6.26	7.6	7.46	8.26	9.6	9.43	10.26
Woodcombe Lane	2.50	3.7	3.30	3.50	4.10	4.27	4.50	5.10	5.30	5.50	6.10	6.30	7.10	7.50	8.30	9.10	9.47	10.30
Brakeley Steps	2.58	3.15	3.38	3.58	4.18	4.35	4.58	5.18	5.38	5.58	6.18	6.38	7.18	7.58	8.38	9.18	9.55	10.38
Budleigh Hill (for Selworthy)	3.1	3.18	3.41	4.1	4.21	4.38	5.1	5.21	5.41	6.1	6.21	6.41	7.21	8.1	8.41	9.21	9.58	10.41
Allerford	3.4	3.21	3.44	4.4	4.24	4.41	5.4	5.24	5.44	6.4	6.24	6.44	7.24	8.4	8.44	9.24	10.1	10.44
Bossington (Green)		3.26				4.46											10.6	
Newbridge	3.7		3.47	4.7	4.27		5.7	5.27	5.47	6.7	6.27	6.47	7.27	8.7	8.47	9.27		10.47
Porlock	3.10	3.32	3.50	4.10	4.31	4.52	5.10	5.30	5.50	6.10	6.30	6.50	7.30	8.10	8.50	9.30	10.12	10.50
Porlock Weir arr.	3.20	3.42	4.0	4.20	4.40	5.2	5.20	5.40	6.0	6.20	6.40	7.0	7.40	8.20	9.0	9.40	10.22	11.0

	am	am	am	am	am	am	am	am	pm	pm	pm	pm	pm	pm	pm	pm	pm	pm
Porlock Weir dep.	8.7	9.24	10.0	10.25	10.45	11.5	11.25	11.45	12.5	12.25	12.45	1.5	1.25	1.42	2.5	2.25	2.45	3.5
Porlock	8.17	9.31	10.10	10.35	10.55	11.15	11.36	11.55	12.15	12.35	12.55	1.15	1.35	1.52	2.15	2.35	2.55	3.15
Newbridge		9.37	10.13	10.38	10.58	11.18	11.38	11.58	12.18	12.38	12.58	1.18	1.39		2.18	2.38	2.58	3.18
Bossington (Green)	8.23													1.58				
Allerford	8.28	9.40	10.16	10.41	11.1	11.21	11.41	12.1	12.21	12.41	1.1	1.21	1.41	2.3	2.21	2.41	3.1	3.21
Budleigh Hill (for Selworthy)	8.31	9.43	10.19	10.44	11.4	11.24	11.44	12.4	12.24	12.44	1.4	1.24	1.44	2.6	2.24	2.44	3.4	3.24
Brakeley Steps	8.34	9.46	10.22	10.47	11.7	11.27	11.47	12.7	12.27	12.47	1.7	1.27	1.47	2.9	2.27	2.47	3.7	3.27
Woodcombe Lane	8.42	9.54	10.30	10.55	11.15	11.35	11.55	12.15	12.35	12.55	1.15	1.35	1.55	2.17	2.35	2.55	3.15	3.35
Minehead (Square)	8.45	9.57	10.33	10.58	11.18	11.38	11.58	12.18	12.38	12.58	1.18	1.38	1.58	2.20	2.38	2.58	3.18	3.38
Minehead (Railway Station) arr.	8.47	9.59	10.35	11.0	11.20	11.40	12.0	12.20	12.40	1.0	1.20	1.40	2.0	2.22	2.40	3.0	3.20	3.40

	pm	pm	pm	pm	pm	pm	pm	pm	pm	pm	pm	pm	pm	pm	pm	pm	pm	pm
Porlock Weir dep.	3.25	3.45	4.5	4.25	4.45	5.5	5.25	5.45	6.5	6.22	6.45	7.5	7.45	8.25	9.5	9.45	10.25	11.0
Porlock	3.35	3.55	4.15	4.36	4.55	5.15	5.35	5.50	6.15	6.42	6.55	7.15	7.55	8.35	9.15	9.55	10.35	11.10
Newbridge	3.38	3.58	4.18	4.38	4.58	5.18	5.38	5.58	6.18		6.58	7.18	7.58	8.38	9.18	9.58	10.38	11.13
Bossington (Green)										6.38								
Allerford	3.41	4.1	4.21	4.41	5.1	5.21	5.41	6.1	6.21	6.43	7.1	7.21	8.1	8.41	9.21	10.1	10.41	11.16
Budleigh Hill (for Selworthy)	3.44	4.4	4.24	4.44	5.4	5.24	5.44	6.4	6.24	6.46	7.4	7.24	8.4	8.44	9.24	10.4	10.44	11.19
Brakeley Steps	3.47	4.7	4.27	4.47	5.7	5.27	5.47	6.7	6.27	6.49	7.7	7.27	8.7	8.47	9.27	10.7	10.47	11.22
Woodcombe Lane	3.55	4.15	4.35	4.55	5.15	5.35	5.55	6.15	6.35	6.57	7.15	7.35	8.15	8.55	9.35	10.15	10.55	11.30
Minehead (Square)	3.58	4.18	4.38	4.58	5.18	5.38	5.58	6.18	6.38	7.0	7.18	7.38	8.18	8.58	9.38	10.18	10.58	11.33
Minehead (Railway Station) arr.	4.0	4.20	4.40	5.0	5.20	5.40	6.0	6.20	6.40	7.2	7.20	7.40	8.20	9.0	9.40	10.20	11.0	11.35

Sunday Service

15th JUNE to 14th SEPTEMBER, 1952, inclusive.

	am	am	pm	pm	pm	pm	pm	pm	pm	pm	pm	pm	pm	pm	pm	pm	pm	pm
Minehead (Railway Station) dep.	9.25	10.45	12.25	1.5	1.45	2.25	3.5	3.45	4.25	5.5	5.45	6.25	7.5	7.45	8.25	9.5	9.45	10.25
Minehead (W. N Office or Square)	9.26	10.46	12.26	1.6	1.46	2.26	3.6	3.46	4.26	5.6	5.46	6.26	7.6	7.46	8.26	9.6	9.46	10.26
Woodcombe Lane	9.30	10.50	12.30	1.10	1.50	2.30	3.10	3.50	4.30	5.10	5.47	6.30	7.10	7.50	8.30	9.10	9.50	10.30
Brakeley Steps	9.38	10.58	12.38	1.18	1.50	2.38	3.18	3.58	4.38	5.18	5.55	6.38	7.18	7.58	8.38	9.18	9.58	10.38
Budleigh Hill (for Selworthy)	9.41	11.1	12.41	1.21	2.1	2.41	3.21	4.1	4.41	5.21	5.58	6.41	7.21	8.1	8.41	9.21	10.1	10.41
Allerford	9.44	11.4	12.44	1.24	2.4	2.44	3.24	4.4	4.44	5.24	6.1	6.44	7.24	8.4	8.44	9.24	10.4	10.44
Bossington (Green)											6.6							
Newbridge	9.47	11.7	12.47	1.27	2.7	2.47	3.27	4.7	4.47	5.27		6.47	7.27	8.7	8.47	9.27	10.7	10.47
Porlock	9.50	11.10	12.50	1.30	2.10	2.50	3.30	4.10	4.50	5.30	6.12	6.50	7.30	8.10	8.50	9.30	10.10	10.50
Porlock Weir arr.	10.0	11.20	1.0	1.40	2.20	3.0	3.40	4.20	5.0	5.40	6.22	7.0	7.40	8.20	9.0	9.40	10.20	11.0

	am	am	pm	pm	pm	pm	pm	pm	pm	pm	pm	pm	pm	pm	pm	pm	pm	pm
Porlock Weir dep.	10.5	11.25	1.5	1.42	2.25	3.5	3.45	4.25	5.5	5.45	6.25	7.5	7.45	8.25	9.5	9.45	10.20	11.0
Porlock	10.15	11.35	1.15	1.52	2.35	3.15	3.55	4.35	5.15	5.55	6.35	7.15	7.55	8.35	9.15	9.55	10.30	11.10
Newbridge	10.18	11.38	1.18		2.39	3.18	3.58	4.38	5.18	5.58	6.38	7.18	7.58	8.38	9.18	9.58	10.33	11.13
Bossington (Green)				1.58														
Allerford	10.21	11.41	1.21	2.3	2.41	3.21	4.1	4.41	5.21	6.1	6.41	7.21	8.1	8.41	9.21	10.1	10.36	11.16
Budleigh Hill (for Selworthy)	10.24	11.44	1.24	2.6	2.44	3.24	4.4	4.44	5.24	6.4	6.44	7.24	8.4	8.44	9.24	10.4	10.39	11.19
Brakeley Steps	10.27	11.47	1.27	2.9	2.47	3.27	4.7	4.47	5.27	6.7	6.47	7.27	8.7	8.47	9.27	10.7	10.42	11.22
Woodcombe Lane	10.35	11.55	1.35	2.17	2.55	3.35	4.15	4.55	5.35	6.15	6.55	7.35	8.15	8.55	9.35	10.15	10.50	11.30
Minehead (Square)	10.38	11.58	1.38	2.20	2.58	3.38	4.18	4.58	5.38	6.18	6.58	7.38	8.18	8.58	9.38	10.18	10.53	11.33
Minehead (Railway Station) arr.	10.40	12.0	1.40	2.22	3.0	3.40	4.20	5.0	5.40	6.20	7.0	7.40	8.20	9.0	9.40	10.20	10.55	11.35

The Company will not be responsible for any delay in connection with this Service.

Parcels taken at owner's risk.   Passenger's Luggage conveyed.

All Communications to be addressed to the Manager, Blue Motors.

For any other information apply to the Company's Servants.

COX, MINEHEAD

Blue Motors timetable for 1952.

Fares

Through fares from Minehead (Railway Station):

	1934		1951	
	Single	Return	Single	Return
Minehead W.N. Office or Square			1½d	
Woodcombe Lane	2d		2½d	
Brakeley Steps	4d	8d	4½d	
Budleigh Hill	5d	9d	5½d	10d
Allerford	6d	10d	7d	
Bossington, Green			8d	1/1d
Newbridge	6d	10d	7d	11d
Porlock	7d	1/–	8d	1/1d
West Porlock	8d	1/2d		
Porlock Weir	9d	1/3d	10d	1/5d

Through fares from Porlock Weir:

	1934		1951	
	Single	Return	Single	Return
Porlock	2d	3d	2½d	
Newbridge			3½d	
Bossington, Green			4½d	
Allerford	4d	8d	4½d	
Budleigh Hill	5d	9d	5½d	10d
Brakeley Steps	6d	10d	7d	11d
Woodcombe Lane			9d	
Minehead, Square			10d	
Minehead, Railway Station			10d	1/5d

1934, PICTURE BUS, available only on buses
departing from Porlock Weir between 5.30 pm
and 7.15 pm.

	Return
Porlock Weir to Minehead	10d
Porlock	9d
Allerford and Budleigh Hill	7d

Unemployed (Fridays) 8d Return.

Tickets

The tickets used by the Company were usually printed by Williamson, Printer, Ashton, although some had no printer's name on them. They were cancelled by a bell punch of the Williamson make. Return tickets were often cancelled with ticket nippers, the pattern of which varied. Some marks were like a letter M on its side, others had a V shape.

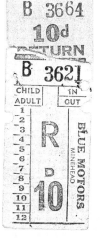

Nos 1 and 2 are ordinary single tickets. No 3 is a type of return ticket, as used up until about 1950. No 4 is a return ticket of the later type, which had the top torn off for the return journey. No 5 is an exchange ticket, issued in exchange for a Western National return ticket, used on a Blue Motors' bus for the return journey.

The Company issued small booklets containing twelve white coloured workman's cheap tickets. These tickets were about the size of a whole return ticket placed horizontal (there being one for each journey on each weekday, one being lettered Forward Journey and the other Return Journey for each day). These were stapled together between two light brown covers, the top cover had the full registered name of the Company along with its name, address and telephone number at the top, then came the wording:

12 Workman's Cheap Tickets
available between ....
and MINEHEAD
Week commencing ....

At the Company's office there was a roll of tickets, usually on a shelf behind the counter. They were ordinary small tickets without the Company's name printed on them. I believe they were valued 6d. They were all numbered and were dark mauve in colour, their most likely use was as Parcels tickets.

Left: a ticket of the type used when the stock of usual tickets ran out.
Right: a Western National exchange ticket, issued in exchange for a Blue Motors' return ticket on a return journey.

4

Excursions and Tours

From the early days of the Company, tours have been operated to various places of interest. An Excursions and Tours licence was issued after the 1930 Road Traffic Act came into effect, to operate coach tours from Minehead. The departure place was at North Road, opposite the Company's garage, and the picking up points were at Porlock, Dunster, Dunster Beach, and Alcombe.

The booking office at Minehead was the Company's office at 39 The Avenue, (telephone Minehead 75). In front of the office was a forecourt with room to park a coach – one was usually parked there during the morning, and sometimes during the afternoon if one was available. There were usually several advertisement boards standing outside, these being painted in white and blue colours. Many had glass fronts and included in the advertisements were several picture post cards of places of interest connected with the particular tour being advertised. There had been different Booking Offices at Porlock, these are mentioned earlier on. The last one was at the Central Garage (telephone Porlock 24). This garage is situated along by the main street near the Porlock Weir end of the village, on the right hand side. There was usually a display of advertisement boards outside but there is no mention of this booking office on the 1949 tours list. However, from lists published after 1951 onwards, it is mentioned on each list. The Company usually had a new Tours list printed each year, these were in the form of a leaflet available at the booking offices.

During the early days (continuing on through the 1920s and part of the 1930s) the tours were operated by char-a-bancs, these being of various makes including Austin, Daimler, Karrier, Crossley and Lancia. Their seating capacities ranged from 14 to 32 passengers. There were also two Albions with Harris 26-seat 'Open' coachwork. These all had a fabric hood which could be folded back on fine days making them completely open on top. During the 1930s several coaches were bought, these gradually replacing the char-a-bancs. These coaches

YB 5914, was an Albion with Harris 'Open' coachwork operating a tour typical of the 1920s and 1930s. It is seen at Cheddar Gorge, Somerset.

Another view of Cheddar Gorge, this time from a more unusual position looking up the Gorge with CYC 463, an AEC Regal coach coming down. The view was taken in the late 1930s and the centre of the roof is open with the fabric section folded back.

A view taken outside of the office at 39 The Avenue, Minehead. CYB 715 is the coach being used to advertise the tours, it has the words EXCURSION & TOUR displayed on its destination blind. (Note the advertisement boards.) The man is Mr Fred Passmore, a conductor who sometimes helped out in the office. A view taken on 11 June 1952.

A view looking into the garage at North Road, Minehead. The coach in the foreground is DYC 20, a Leyland Cheetah. Just visible on this view taken on 11 June 1952 is JYD 199.

were of various makes including several of Albion manufacture, and included Victor and Valkyrie models, with Duple and Thomas Harrington coachwork seating 20 to 30 persons. There was also a Dennis Lancet 2, with Dennis Bros Ltd coachwork, and an AEC Regal with Thomas Harrington coachwork, both seating 32 persons. There was also a Leyland Lion, and three Leyland Cheetahs, seating ranged from 28 to 32 passengers. The Leyland Cheetahs did not use Porlock Hill, but were driven via the Toll road instead. Between 1939 and 1945 all coach tours were suspended.

After the war years more new coaches arrived, firstly of Leyland manufacture. These were the Tiger PS1 and PS2 models, seating 33 persons, the former having Thomas Harrington coachwork and the latter having a full front H V Burlingham Ltd body. There were also the Thomas Harrington 29-seat coaches of the Comet normal control type, and the Lion with its new 31-seat coachwork on a 1937 chassis. Later three new Bedford SBs entered service, seating 31, 33 and 35 persons respectively, two having Duple and the remaining one Thomas Harrington coachwork.

It was always a sight to watch the coaches come out of the garage on a summer's day, in particular the Half-Day Tour departures between 2.15 pm and 2.45 pm. Several of the coaches would line up, one behind the other along North Road. Each would have its destination indicator set for the tour it was about to operate and would be immaculate in its appearance, as they always were, the dark blue paintwork and polished chrome lines gleaming in the sunlight.

The drivers had three clean white coats issued for each week. In addition to the tours advertised on the lists there were also special tours operated to special events such as the Bridgwater Fair.

The half-day and evening tour to Selworthy, Bossington, Porlock Weir and Horner Woods was always known as the 'Old World Villages' tour.

Excursions and Tours, Summer 1953
Day Tours

	Depart		Fare
Daily	10.15	LYNMOUTH AND DOONE VALLEY, via Porlock, Watersmeet Rockford, Brenden and Malmsmead. Lynmouth 2½ hours.	8/6
Daily	10.00	GLASTONBURY, WELLS AND CHEDDAR, via Bridgwater, Glastonbury, and Wells. Glastonbury ½ hour – Wells 1½ hours – Cheddar 1½ hours.	11/6
Daily	9.45	ILFRACOMBE, via Lynmouth and Combe Martin. Returning via Simonsbath and Exford. Lynmouth ½ hour – Ilfracombe 3 hours.	11/6
Daily	9.30	CLOVELLY, via Simonsbath, Barnstaple and Bideford. Returning via Bideford, Barnstaple and South Molton. Barnstaple ½ hour – Clovelly 2 hours – South Molton 1 hour.	13/6
Mon. Wed.	9.30	TORQUAY, via Exe Valley, Tiverton, Exeter, Dawlish and Teignmouth. Returning via Exeter and Tiverton. Tiverton ¼ hour – Torquay 2 hours – Exeter 1 hour.	13/-
Tues.	10.00	SIDMOUTH, via Taunton and Blagdon. Returning via Tiverton and Exe Valley. Sidmouth 2 hours – Exeter 1 hour.	11/6
Tues.	10.00	WESTON-SUPER-MARE, via Burnham-on-Sea; allowing five hours' stay.	9/6
Wed.	10.00	OVER EXMOOR, via Porlock, Glenthorne, Lynmouth. Return via Watersmeet, Simonsbath, Winsford Hill, Tarr Steps, and Dulverton and Exe Valley. Lynmouth 2½ hours – Watersmeet ½ hour – Tarr Steps ½ hour – Dulverton ¾ hour.	10/-
Thurs.	9.30	WEYMOUTH, via Crewkerne and Dorchester. Return via Dorchester and Yeovil. Weymouth 2½ hours – Yeovil ½ hour.	13/6
Thurs.	9.30	HUNTER'S INN AND WOOLACOMBE SANDS, via Lynmouth. Returning via Simonsbath. Lynmouth ½ hour – Hunter's Inn 1¼ hours – Woolacombe Sands 1½ hours.	13/-
Fri.	9.30	BUCKFAST ABBEY, allowing two hours' stay; returning via Newton Abbot and Exeter, one hour for tea.	13/6
Sat.	9.30	BRISTOL, allowing five hours' stay. Drop at Zoo or Anchor Road.	8/6

The following tours are only operated on selected days as advertised at office.

9.30	SIDMOUTH AND EXMOUTH, via Taunton and Honiton. Returning via Exmouth, Exeter, and Exe Valley. Sidmouth 1½ hours – Exmouth 1½ hours.	13/6
10.00	LYME REGIS, via Taunton and Chard. Returning via Tiverton and Exe Valley. Chard ¼ hour – Lyme Regis 2 hours – Tiverton 1 hour.	11/6
9.00	RIVER DART, via Tiverton, Exeter, Newton Abbot, Totnes. Return via Paignton and Torquay.	13/–
9.00	LONGLEAT HOUSE, via Glastonbury, Shepton Mallet. Return via Bath and Bridgwater, allowing 2¼ hours at Longleat – 1 hour at Bath.	13/–
9.00	DARTMOOR, via Haytor and Widecombe-in-the-Moor. Tiverton ¼ hour – Haytor ¼ hour – Widecombe 1 hour – Exeter ¾ hour.	16/–
9.00	BOURNEMOUTH, via Ilminster, Yeovil, Sherborne and Blandford. Returning via Dorchester, Crewkerne, Ilminster and Taunton. Yeovil ¼ hour – Bournemouth 2½ hours – Crewkerne ¼ hour.	16/–

HALF-DAY TOURS

2.30	LYNMOUTH AND DOONE VALLEY, via Porlock, County Gate and Countisbury. Returning via Brenden and Malmsmead.	7/6
2.30	OVER DUNKERY (the highest point on Exmoor), via Wheddon Cross and Dunkery Hill Gate. Returning via Webber's Post and Horner Woods.	4/6
2.30	LYNMOUTH AND EXMOOR, via Porlock. Returning via Simonsbath and Exford.	7/6
2.30	MOORLAND TOUR. Over Exmoor, via Wheddon Cross, Exford, Chetsford Water. Returning via Porlock and Horner Woods.	6/–
2.30	TARR STEPS, via Winsford, Winsford Hill and Dulverton. Returning via the Exe Valley.	7/6
2.30	QUANTOCK HILLS, via Blue Anchor, St Audries and Holford Glen. Returning via Crowcombe.	6/6
2.30	CROYDON HILLS, LUXBOROUGH VALLEY, HORNER WOODS.	5/6
2.30	WINSFORD HILL AND DULVERTON, via Winsford Hill. Returning via the Exe Valley.	7/6
2.30	MOORLAND TOUR, via Withypool, Sandway, Molland Common, Dulverton. Returning via Bury Hill and Heathpoult.	8/–
2.45	SELWORTHY, Bossington, Porlock Weir and Horner Woods.	3/6
Sunday 2.15	WOOKEY HOLE CAVES, via Glastonbury.	8/6
Sunday 2.15	CHEDDAR CAVES.	8/6
Sunday 2.15	WESTON-SUPER-MARE. Allowing 2 hours.	8/–

PYB 383, was a Bedford SB, with Duple coachwork, seen parked in North Road, Minehead during early evening after it had arrived back from operating a tour.

JYC 855, was a Leyland Tiger PS1, parked in the car and coach park at Lynmouth whilst on a Half Day Tour. This coach was one of those used to operate the Holiday Tours and was known to have operated the North and Central Wales Tour during 1953.

OVER DUNKERY. Via Wheddon Cross and Dunkery Hill Gate.
Returning via Horner Woods.   3/6

CROYDON HILLS AND LUXBOROUGH VALLEY.   4/-

BRENDON HILLS. Via Timberscombe and Raleigh's Cross.
Returning via Stiklepath and Washford.   4/-

ST AUDRIES. Via Carhampton, Blue Anchor.
Returning via Williton and Washford.   3/6

SELWORTHY, BOSSINGTON, PORLOCK AND HORNER WOODS.   3/-

The Company reserve the right to cancel any advertised Tour should there be insufficient passengers, to alter the route of any Tour and time of departure should circumstances demand, but the times and routes will be adhered to as far as possible. Although every endeavour will be made by the Company to keep to the seats marked off, there is no guarantee given or implied.

On the 1952 list of Day Tours only was:–

9.30   EXETER direct. Allowing five hours.   9/-

Above left
Left to right: Drivers Mr Tom
Bowden and Mr Bill Manley
with Mildred Rayment. Next
is Driver Mr Frank Bryant,
stood by one of the coaches. It
is most likely one of the Albion
Victors with Thomas
Harrington coachwork seen in
July 1942.

Bottom left
A general view taken outside
of the office at The Avenue,
Minehead. The driver is Mr
Eric Tarr and the coach is
PYA 973.

5

British Holiday Tours and Private Hire

The first year these tours were operated is believed to have been 1951. During that year there was a folded advertisement paper issued advertising two tours, both for seven days, firstly to North and Central Wales, and secondly to Lancashire and Lake District. Both were priced at twelve guineas. No specific dates of departure are given and on the front it states that these tours are operated from Minehead and Porlock, between March and October inclusive, depart Sundays – Porlock Church – 8.40 am, Minehead (North Road) 9.00 am.

For the 1953 season the company issued a very smart booklet introducing a new additional tour to Scotland for 13 days. It also included a weekend tour to Blackpool Illuminations for three days, which had been previously operated but not listed with the Holiday Tours, as well as the two previously mentioned tours. Only the Minehead departure place and times are given, Porlock not being mentioned. The 1953 prices and dates of departure are given below:

SCOTLAND £32.0.0d
Mondays: 18 May and 14 September

NORTH AND CENTRAL WALES £14.10.0d
Sundays: 10 May and 20 September

LANCASHIRE & LAKE DISTRICT £14.10.0d
Sundays: 24 May and 27 September

BLACKPOOL ILLUMINATIONS £3.10.0d
Fridays: 9, 16 and 23 October

The above tours were advertised for 1954, with an additional tour introduced, SOUTH COAST, 7 days, £14.0.0d.

The driver of CYB 715 which was used to operate the September 1951 Holiday Tour to Lancashire and the Lake District was Mr T Bracegirdle, who I understand encouraged the start of these tours. He undertook it because he knew the area. Another driver, Mr T I Sparkes, was a passenger on this tour who was then able to get to know the route so that he could drive it later on.

CYB 715, was a Leyland Lion, with 31-seat Thomas Harrington coachwork waiting to set off on a 7-day Holiday Tour to Lancashire and the Lake District during September 1951. Stood by it are the Company's Manager, Mr G F R Sandford (extreme left), Driver, Mr T Bracegirdle (kneeling down), and the passengers who include Mr T I Sparkes, a Company driver (fourth from left), Mr Charlie Babb, the garage Foreman (fourth from right with cap), and Mr Bill Martin, a local bus driver (extreme right). The view was taken near the Polo Field, Dunster.

The vehicles used to operate these tours were CYB 715, the Leyland Lion, by now with a new body seating 31 passengers, built by Thomas Harrington and JYC 855 and JYD 199, both Leyland Tiger PS1s with 33-seat Thomas Harrington coachwork.

The North and Central Wales tour was operated by JYD 199 on 10 May 1953, and by JYC 855 on 20 September 1953.

Mr Eric Tarr remembered that on one occasion he drove MYA 121, Leyland Tiger PS2, with 33-seat full front H V Burlingham coachwork, on the Blackpool Illuminations tour. This coach was not used to take the passengers along to view the Illuminations, but a coach was hired from a local firm at Blackpool for this purpose.

MYA 121 was a Leyland Tiger PS2, parked at Porlock Weir and waiting there whilst on an Old World Villages Tour. This is an afternoon tour calling at several villages between Minehead and Horner Woods. It is seen (on 14 September 1952) parked alongside the wall just in front of the place where the bus service journeys commence.

A view of a party of pupils with Mr Gibbs, the Headmaster, on the right, taken outside of Minehead Grammar School. The coach would be an Albion Victor with Thomas Harrington coachwork. The original print is in the West Somerset Museum, Allerford, and is reproduced here by courtesy of Mrs M Freeman-Archer.

Private Hire was an important part of the business. Coaches were hired by various parties, they were also sometimes hired to the Royal Blue Express Coaching business.

Mr Francis Freegard, who was a conductor during the late 1930s. Fleet No 14 can be seen on part of the coach behind him, CYC 463, an AEC Regal.

One of the Crossley char-a-bancs, a view taken during a visit to Cheddar.

Driver Mr Sid Ward with one of the Thomas Harrington-bodied Leyland Tigers seen on an Over Dunkery tour.

A view of the back of Crossley char-a-banc YA 3077. It is receiving some attention to a rear wheel. (Note the firm's fleet name with Porlock & Minehead painted on it, also the Hackney Carriage plate showing the vehicle to be a 14-seater.)

EYA 923, was a Leyland Cheetah, with Thomas Harrington coachwork. It is seen during the wartime parked at the service departure place, Minehead Railway Station. (Note the wartime headlamp shades and the white flash on each front mudguard.) *Photo: S L Poole – Courtesy, Alan Cross.*

Mr Charlie Babb, Foreman and Engineer seen with Mr Tom Bowden, Bus Driver, each of these men gave over thirty years service to the Blue Motors, they are stood in front of HYB 676, AEC, Regal with Thomas Harrington bodywork. *Photo by courtesy of Mr E A Bowden.*

AEC Regal HYB 676, with
Thomas Harrington
bodywork. It is seen parked
opposite the Railway Station,
Minehead, waiting to depart
for Porlock Weir on 6 August
1952. *Courtesy Alan Cross.*

A view taken at Cheddar with
Driver Mr Sam Hooper and
the passengers stood by one of
the Leyland Tigers with
Thomas Harrington
coachwork. *Photo courtesy Mr
E A Bowden.*

Appendix 1

Abbreviations:

In front of the seating capacity

B – Service Bus.   Ch – Char-a-banc.   C – Coach.   OC – Coach with Fabric Hood.
W – Waggonette.   UB – Wartime Utility Bus Body.   FC – Full front Coach.

Following the seating capacity

S – Several entrances.   F – Front entrance.
R – Rear entrance.   C – Central entrance.

Appendix 1

The Porlock Weir, Porlock and Minehead Motor Services Company Limited
Blue Motors, Minehead – List of Vehicles

Reg	Make	Model	Chassis	Body	Builder	From	To
Y 401	Napier	25 hp		Ch22		6/16	8/19
Y 4318	Maudslay	25/30 hp		W11R		7/16	
Y 4265	Karrier	50 hp	1340	B35S		7/16	/27
Y 4618	Austin	25 hp		Ch18		5/17	
Y 6187	Daimler	22 hp		Ch23S	A G Dowell	8/19	
Y 7665	Karrier	50 hp		Ch28		8/20	
XB 9780	Karrier			Ch28S			
YA 2828	Crossley	X	11060	Ch14		3/22	/28
YA 3077	Crossley	25 hp		Ch14		4/22	
YA 4003	Crossley	X	10975	Ch14		8/22	8/29
AR 9306	Karrier			Ch32		/23	/27
YA 6600	Lancia	35 hp	Z.4694	Ch 19S		7/23	6/34
YB 5914	Albion	PN 26	5005F	OC26F	Harris	4/26	9/39
YB 5915	Albion	PN 26	5006H	OC26F	Harris	4/26	9/39
YC 599	Albion	PK 26	5043A	B29F	Duple	7/27	9/39
YC 3473	Lancia	35 hp	2009	Ch20		6/28	7/36
YC 7355	Dennis	GL	70569	B20F	Duple	8/29	
YD 4593	Dennis	Lancet 1	170139	B32R	Duple	4/32	7/40
YD 4700	Dennis	Dart	75781	C20F	Duple	5/32	5/36
YD 7169	Albion	Victor PH 49	15006A	C20	Duple	5/33	3/42
YD 9697	Dennis	Lancet 1	170666	B32F	Duple	5/34	/40
AYC 106	Albion	Victor PK 115	25002D	C26C	Thos Harrington	4/35	6/48
AYC 107	Albion	Victor PK 115	25002E	C26C	Thos Harrington	4/35	5/50
BYC 341	Albion	Victor PK 115	25008L	C20C	Thos Harrington	4/36	5/51
BYC 698	Albion	Valkyrie	44001J	C30C	Thos Harrington	6/36	9/39
BYD 178	Dennis	Lancet 2	175115	C32	Dennis Bros Ltd	8/36	7/40
CYB 715	Leyland	Lion LT7	13785	C28F	Thos Harrington	3/37	
CYC 463	AEC	Regal	6622166	C32F	Thos Harrington	5/37	7/44
DYC 20	Leyland	Cheetah LZ2	200241	C31F	Thos Harrington	6/38	2/53
EYA 923	Leyland	Cheetah LZ2	201440	C32F	Thos Harrington	3/39	8/53
EYB 488	Leyland	Cheetah LZ2	201381	C32F	Thos Harrington	5/39	2/53
GYA 598	Bedford	OWB	20492	UB32F	Duple	6/44	1/52
HYB 676	AEC	Regal	06625009	B35F	Thos Harrington	12/46	6/53
JYB 168	Dennis	Lancet 3	283J3	B35F	Thos Harrington	10/47	6/53
GC 4823	AEC	Regal	662183	C32R	Thos Harrington	/48	/48
JYC 855	Leyland	Tiger PS1	472198	C33F	Thos Harrington	3/48	
JYD 199	Leyland	Tiger PS1	472199	C33F	Thos Harrington	4/48	
LYD 581	Leyland	Comet CPP1	495225	C29F	Thos Harrington	5/50	
MYA 121	Leyland	Tiger PS2	500075	FC33F	H V Burlingham	6/50	
MYA 246	Leyland	Comet CPP1	495240	C29F	Thos Harrington	6/50	
NYC 993	Bedford	SB	6584	C31F	Duple	2/52	
PYA 973	Bedford	SB	16955	C33F	Thos Harrington	5/53	
PYB 383	Bedford	SB	17060	C35F	Duple	6/53	

Y 401	Acquired from Messrs Hardy and Co, Minehead. It was originally registered on 19 April 1916.
Y 6187	It had its second body fitted to it by the time the photograph in this book was taken.
YA 2828	Chassis acquired from the Government. Registered on 22 March 1922.
YA 3077	Chassis acquired from the Government. Registered on 13 April 1922.
YA 4003	Chassis acquired from the Government. Registered on 4 August 1922.
AR 9306	Ex Blue Belle.
YA 6600	Chassis had previously been owned by the Government (War Department). Registered on 25 July 1923. The last licence for it expired on 30 September 1934.
YC 599	The seating capacity reduced to 26 during 1930s.
YC 3473	The last licence expired on 30 September 1936.
YC 7355	The last licence issued expired on 1 October 1939, by then it was with another owner.
YD 4593	It had Duple body No 2862.
YD 4700	It had Duple body No 2957. Registered on 10 May 1932.
BYD 178	A refund was made for the last licence on 5 July 1940.
CYB 715	Was latter fitted with new coachwork by Thomas Harrington C31F, body No 708 by June 1950.
CYC 463	A refund was made for the last licence on 13 July 1944.
DYC 20	The seating capacity changed to 27, 2/50.
EYA 923	The seating capacity changed to 27, 2/50.
EYB 488	The seating capacity changed to 22.
GYA 598	It had Duple body No 38814. It was later UB30F.
GC 4823	Ex the Government (War Department) No 1260847. It was originally new to Messrs Timpsons, Catford, No 203 in March 1930.
JYC 855	It had body No 303.
JYD 199	It had body No 313.
LYD 581	It had body No 754.
MYA 121	It had body No 4528.
MYA 246	It had body No 792.
NYC 993	It had Duple body No 57512.
PYA 973	It had body No 1202.

Disposals

Y 401	To a London owner.
Y 4265	To a Southport owner, and scrapped.
Y 4618	To a London owner.
Y 6187	To a Wallasey owner, by 12/28.
YA 4003	To F H Harrison, Minehead, Somerset. It was last licensed 9/30.
YA 6600	Sold for scrap.
YB 5914	To Somerset County Council. Ambulance 9/39 to 12/41.
YB 5915	To Axbridge Rural District Council. Fire Tender 9/39 to 12/41. It was returned to the company by 1945 and withdrawn at an unknown date.
YC 599	To Somerset County Council. Ambulance until 12/43.
YC 3473	To Albion Motors, dealers, then to Stone, St Audries, Somerset.
YC 7355	To C J Walling, Eastergate, Sussex.
YD 4593	Requisitioned by the Government, circa 7/40. WD No M4138798.
YD 4700	To Messrs Hawkins Bros, Minehead, Somerset by 1937. It was later War Department No M1260696.

YD 7169	To Mr E G Bryant, Williton, Somerset.
YD 9697	Requisitioned by the Government. (War Department.)
AYC 106	To Mrs W A Hart, Hart's Bus Service, Budleigh Salterton, Devon.
AYC 107	To Mr Bond, Appledore, Devon.
BYC 341	To J W J Johns Esq, Woodford Bridge, Milton Dameral, Devon.
BYC 698	Requisitioned by the Government. It was later with Messrs Dodds and Company, Troon, Scotland.
BYD 178	Requisitioned by the Government.
CYC 463	Requisitioned by the Government.
DYC 20	To Chard and District Coaches, (branch of Wessex Motorways), Chard, Somerset.
EYA 923	To A E Sherrin, Carhampton, Somerset.
EYB 488	To Chard and District Coaches, (branch of Wessex Motorways), Chard, Somerset.
GYA 598	To C & E Motors Ltd, Coventry. It was later owned by the Rover Co Ltd, Solihull.
HYB 676	To Western National Omnibus Co Ltd, Exeter, Devon.
JYB 168	To Western National Omnibus Co Ltd.

All other coaches not shown as withdrawn on the second page of the main fleet list were transferred to Scarlet and Blue Motor Coaches Ltd, April 1954.

Appendix 2

List of Motor Cars

Y 2573	Ford	20 hp	4 seats	Black*	15 cwt	1/17	3/20
Y 5265	Ford	15 hp		Black	Under 1 ton	2/19	
Y 8858	Overland	16/18 hp		Green	1 ton 16 cwt	7/20	
HU	Armstrong Siddeley						/29
HU 8108	Armstrong Siddeley 7563		8 seats				/39
PJ 3299	Austin Taxi		5 seats				

Notes

Y 2573   was ex Mr J W Willis, Prospect House, Porlock, Somerset, it was originally registered on 18 June 1914. *Colour changed to Brown by 3/20.

It was later passed on to Messrs Yandle and Sons Ltd, Silver Street, Ilminster, Somerset, then on to Mr Tom Parris, George Inn, Chardstock, Chard, Somerset.

Y 8858   was a Landaulette.

HU 8108   had a PSV licence issued. On 29 November 1939 this car was licenced to Mr F Knight, 60 Orchard Street, Weston-super-Mare.

PJ 3299   had a PSV licence issued.

Appendix 3
Destination Blinds

The following is a copy in the correct order of the names on the complete destination blind of No JYD 199. (Note that the bus service names are first with the exception of Porlock Weir, which is last.) If the coach was used on the bus service journeys it would mean an almost complete turn of the whole destination blind for the return journey.

PORLOCK

MINEHEAD

DUPLICATE

PRIVATE

ALL DAY TOUR

HALF DAY TOUR

EVENING TOUR

TO THE MEET

WOOKEY HOLE
& CHEDDAR

CHEDDAR CAVES

WOOKEY HOLE CAVE

LYNMOUTH (DIRECT)

LYNMOUTH &
DOONE VALLEY

CLOVELLY

ILFRACOMBE

HUNTERS INN
& WOOLACOMBE

OVER EXMOOR

SIDMOUTH

TORQUAY

LYME REGIS

OVER DARTMOOR

BUCKFAST ABBEY

SIDMOUTH
& EXMOUTH

WESTON SUPER MARE

MOORLAND TOUR

QUANTOCK HILLS

OVER BRENDON HILLS

THE OLD WORLD
VILLAGES

COTHELSTONE

TARR STEPS

OVER DUNKERY

DOONE VALLEY
& OARE CHURCH

CROYDON HILLS

ST. AUDRIES

WEYMOUTH

BOURNEMOUTH

PORLOCK WEIR

The letters of the single words on one line are fairly large and those where there are two lines are both slightly smaller than half of the large size letter. The only exception to the large single words was that of Weston-super-Mare. Here the first and last words are large size and the centre word is written in small size letters: there is no hyphen in between the name on the actual destination blind.

The following names were noted displayed on the destination blind of HYB 676, the AEC Regal service bus:

PORLOCK

MINEHEAD
VIA BOSSINGTON

PORLOCK WEIR

MINEHEAD

PORLOCK WEIR
VIA BOSSINGTON

DUPLICATE

PRIVATE

EXCURSION

(note the inclusion of via Bossington on some destinations). The correct sequence of the names is not known, the only two actually noted next to each other were Minehead, which was followed by Porlock Weir via Bossington.

Appendix 4

Staff
(Some of the pre 1939 staff)

Manager: F J Loveless, by January 1917 Thomas Priscott, to 1921. F J Stoate, from 1921.
Foreman: Charlie Babb.
Office: Ted Willis, Minehead. Frank Norman, Ernest Bowden, Porlock.
Drivers:

	Frank Radford	Bus	Drove No Y 4265. Left c 1920.
	Thomas Bowden	Bus	Started c 1920, retired February 1952.
	William Manley	Bus	Had been a char-a-banc driver.
	Richard Boyle	Bus	Driver by August 1938.
	Sam Hooper	Coach	Had been a char-a-banc driver.
	Frank Bryant	Coach	
	Peter Quinn	Coach	
	Charlie Headford	Coach	
	Harry Creech		Drove Crossley char-a-bancs.
	Jack Everett		
	Fred Prole		
	Tom Burge		Char-a-banc driver.
	Tom Taylor		Hire car driver, seasonal only.

Conductors:

	Edgar Ward		On 'King of the Road' for a year c.1926.
	Victor Manley		Replaced Mr Edgar Ward on No Y 4265.
	Alfred Fowler		Was later a coach driver.
HH 2145	Ernest Bowden		From Porlock office by August 1938.*
	Sidney Ward		Was later a coach driver c.1946 to 12/1951.*
	Francis Freegard		With the firm for about two years.*

* Called up for military service about 1939

Wartime Conductresses

Miss Brenda (Billie) Strong	Mrs K Willis. Went on to 1951
Miss Sybil Wood*	Miss Rita Middleton

* Was with the company for about six months

Known regular Drivers to vehicles, circa 1950s

Tom Bowden	HYB 676)	shared on a shift basis
Ernie Bowden	HYB 676)	
Peter Quinn	JYB 168	
Sam Hooper	JYC 855	(1st)
T I Sparkes	JYC 855	(2nd)
Sid Ward	EYA 923.	From 4/48 JYD 199. From 6/50 MYA 121. (Left 12/51.)
R T Barsby	JYD 199	By summer 1952.

93

Eric Tarr	BYC 341	Then EYB 488 to 2/53. PYA 973 from 5/53.
J H Day	DYC 20	
Pat Baker	LYD 581	
Alf Fowler	MYA 246	

Some of the staff, Summer 1952

Manager:	G F R Sandford			
Foreman:	Charlie Babb			
Office:	C J Griffiths			
Drivers:		*Badge Issued*		
	Sam Hooper		Coach	Senior Driver
HH 1489	R T Barsby	19.2.35	Coach	
HH 2070	G R Baker	26.4.35	Coach	
HH 8789	E Bowden		Bus	Driver from about 1946
HH 10089	Peter Quinn		Bus	Replacement badge originally licensed 1.7.38.
HH 20069	T Bracegirdle	19.4.49	Coach	Drove on Holiday Tours.
HH 21296	E W Tarr	18.5.50	Coach	
HH 21575	W J Salter		Coach	Replacement badge originally licensed 25.8.45.
HH 22779	J Stokle	19.7.51	Coach	
HH 22905	J H Day	20.8.51	Coach	
	T I Sparkes		Coach	Drove on Holiday Tours.
	Alfred Fowler		Coach	
Conductors:				
HH 9780	E A Jackson	17.9.45		
	Fred Passmore			Sometimes helped out in the office.
Conductress:				
HH 26853	Mrs E D Grant	15.6.51		Replaced Mrs K Willis. Was with the firm about a year.

Also two unknown conductors, Badge numbers HH14451 and HH 14920. Mr John Tako was also a conductor, but it is not certain during which years he worked for the Company. There was a driver 'Pat' Baker, this may have been G R Baker mentioned above. After the date the badge was issued the holder may not have joined the Blue Motors immediately.

Bibliography

Gillham, J.C. *Buses Illustrated* No 4, 'The AEC types' (Ian Allan, April 1950).

Gillham, J.C. *Buses Illustrated* Nos 11 and 13, 'Albion' (Ian Allan, 1952/3).

Townsin, Alan *Buses Illustrated* Nos 21 and 22, 'The Leyland Story' (Ian Allan, 1955).

Wise, G.B. *Bus & Coach Recognition* 'Veteran & Vintage' (Ian Allan, 1989).

Townsin, Alan *Buses Illustrated* No 25, 'The Crossley Story' (Ian Allan, January-March 1956).